I WAS A KAMIKAZE

The Knights of the Divine Wind

I Was a Kamikaze

R. Nagatsuka

Translated from the French
by Nina Rootes

With an introduction
by Pierre Clostermann

NEW ENGLISH LIBRARY
TIMES MIRROR

For my comrades in battle, the heroic suicide-pilots who sacrificed their lives for their country, and for the American sailors who were their victims.

In memory of my mother, who died with my name on her lips.

First published in Great Britain in 1973 by Abelard-Schuman Ltd.
© 1972 Ryuji Nagatsuka, Maurice Toesca and Editions Stock
© This translation by Abelard-Schuman Ltd., 1973

*

FIRST NEL PAPERBACK EDITION APRIL 1974
Reprinted July 1975

*

Conditions of sale: This book is sold subject to the condition that it shall not, by way of trade or otherwise, be lent, re-sold, hired out, or otherwise circulated without the publisher's prior consent in any form of binding or cover other than that in which it is published and without a similar condition including this condition being imposed on the subsequent purchaser.

NEL Books are published by
New English Library Limited from Barnard's Inn, Holborn, London, E.C.1.
Made and printed in Great Britain by Hunt Barnard Printing Ltd., Aylesbury, Bucks.

45001927 6

KAMIKAZE

In their homeland, the Japanese suicide-pilots were known by several different names, though Kamikaze was the commonest and the only one to be used by the Allies.

The origin of the name derives from an historical episode. In 1281, the Mongol invasion fleet was sailing towards the islands of Japan when it was struck and destroyed by a tornado. The people believed that Tenshi, the Son of Heaven, had intervened to save them by unleashing *Kamikaze*, the Divine Wind.

Translator's note

PREFACE

'We do not wish the kamikaze tactics to be described by the term "suicide-attacks".

'Right up until the end, we believed we could outweigh your material and scientific superiority by the force of our moral and spiritual convictions.'

These words were addressed to an American Commission of Enquiry, in 1945, by General Kawabe, commander of kamikaze operations to the Imperial General Staff.

The history of the kamikazes – to use the name by which they are most commonly known – has always fascinated the combatant nations of the West.

My book *Feux du Ciel* (Flames in the Sky), published a few years after the war, contained a chapter entitled 'Under the Sign of the Divine Wind' in which I tried to analyse the mentality of these Japanese pilots by tracing the influence of Shintoism and the traditions of *Bushido* on the Japanese mind, and contrasting this with our own customary responses and way of thought.

This text was translated and published in Japan, where it was much discussed and criticised (the American authorities in Tokyo even went so far as to ban it):

'Our conscience, as civilised beings, can admit the possibility of total sacrifice in its noblest form, in the heat of battle or in a paroxysm of suffering or despair – for example, Max Guedj in Norway, the mortally-wounded Lieutenant Kenan who crashed his fighter plane on the torpedo that was about to disembowel his aircraft carrier *Delattre* on the 11th of May, 1940. . . .

'We can understand those pilots who took off on a desperate mission, almost certain that they would not come out of it

7

alive (the "Fairey Battles" at Maastricht in 1940, for instance), but in which an element of chance or superlative skill might still be able to tip the scales, no matter how heavily weighted against them. And I am certain that a glimmer of hope still flickered in the hearts of such men.

'But how can we understand a total contempt for certain death?'*

Now at last we have the first-hand testimony of one of these men who, freely electing to sacrifice his life, was miraculously snatched from the threshold of death.

Who is this witness – the descedant of the Samurais? An officer of the old school, raised in the Imperialist tradition and with a mind nurtured on *Hakko Ishui*?†

No, simply a dissenting student (and we learn with surprise that such rebels existed in Japan). A pacifist intellectual enamoured of French culture, he was destined for a career as a French teacher until he was caught up in the infernal machinery of war. The whole value of this moving document lies in the fact that it comes, not from the fanatic of fiction, but from a conscientious young man who resigned himself to his duty towards a society whose deeds and decisions he did not always approve.

He explains candidly the psychological steps which led him from profound aversion to the military caste to a willingness to sacrifice his life, and this progression is so incredible, so alien to our own way of thinking, that we are compelled to realise its truth.

In order to place his touching odyssey in time, Nagatsuka has given the historical data on the battles in the Pacific in the form of harangues by his successive chiefs. In these passages, his style changes; he is on the defensive and seeks to justify his behaviour by an account of the military disasters that overwhelmed his country.

Elsewhere, when he speaks of Japan, his beloved country, we discover a sensitive man in whom patriotism does not take the traditional or caricatured form which Westerners often

*For details of some of these exploits see *Flames in the Sky* by Pierre Clostermann, D.F.C., Chatto & Windus, London, 1952. Max Gudje was the famous 'Maurice' of Coastal Command. (*Translator's note.*)

†*Hakko Ishui*: the unification of the eight corners of the world under one roof. This mystical concept was the basis of the political aims of 'The Divine Empire'. (*Translator's note.*)

impute to the kamikaze pilot. It is the love of a wise and harmonious nature reared amongst an exceptionally artistic people, for whom respect, affection and obedience have remained the cardinal virtues.

Now and then, an image flares up, lighting the secret recesses of the soul – the pilot, destined to die, kneels beside his mother and tenderly combs her hair with a little wooden comb. . . .

Nevertheless, every page leads implacably towards the conclusion.

From his carefree school days to the privations of life at the flying school, where they were short of planes, fuel, food supplies and men, Nagatsuka's story is carried along on the flood-tide of events, to the day when he volunteered for the *kamikazes*, together with his comrades.

And then comes his last night, his personal Gethsemane – the doubt, the absurdity of the thing, duty, anguish, all his thoughts whirling in his head as the hours tick away slowly, oh, so slowly! . . .

And when the last day dawns in the grey and lowering sky, his resolution is firm, for he has chosen death out of love for his dear ones.

In the final pages, it is the veritable testimony of a man who delivers himself up naked, who flays himself alive, combining an exceptional sensibility with total and unrelenting honesty towards himself.

When hostilities were ended, the official American and Japanese publications minutely laid out the chronology of events and the horrific balance-sheet of the war. But in all this history of the Japanese-American conflict in the Pacific, a great human document was lacking.

Today, at last, Ryuji Nagatsuka brings us that document.

Pierre Clostermann

Part One

'Till we meet again,' said our
lips, but our eyes said 'Farewell.'

Only *tokusos*, 'aspirant' or cadet pilots, were travelling on the branch line train to Kanamaruhara, a military airfield some thirty-seven miles from Utsunomiya. Instead of a literary work or a treatise on law, every one of these ex-students carried a sword wound up in a piece of cloth! The vivid colours of the wrappings – red, purple, yellow, white, blue – contrasted strongly with the severe black uniforms of scholars. The future pilots were withdrawn into themselves and an uneasy silence reigned in the compartment. I looked for students from the Imperial Universities. There were none. Almost all were from private universities.

Some of them, deeply moved, leaned back in their seats with their eyes closed. No doubt they were thinking of their families, whom they had just left at Utsunomiya station. Others, chin in hand, gazed blankly out of the windows. Although the rainy season was approaching, the sky shed a pure, pristine light over the plain.

At the little station of Kanamaruhara, two cadets were waiting for us. Were they veteran *tokusos*? No, they were not wearing pilots' insignia on their tunics, so they must be members of the Aviation Service Corps.

'Follow me!' said one the them brusquely.

There was no sign of a farm and no cattle about. We were now in a military zone and everything around us took on a new aspect: the yellow *Akatonbos* (Dragonflies), or training planes, lined up in formation, the smell of aircraft fuel, and the eddies of sand whirled into the air by the spinning propellers.

Ten minutes later, we found ourselves in front of the barracks. But our two guides marched rapidly past them. Someone asked: 'Aren't those our quarters?' 'No,' was the only answer vouchsafed him. Soon, we came in sight of the

13

hangars and the runway. *Akatonbos* were taking off one after the other. The pilots, bursting with energy, moved about at a run. It was a very pleasing sight. Suddenly, a pilot came up to me and said: 'Aren't you a student from the Shizuoka High School? I was studying in the third grade there. I'm in the first intake of *tokusos*, so I'll be leaving this flying school in three days' time. . . . Good luck!'

At that time, students from state high schools spoke to each other without formality, even if they did not know each other. This man had recognised me by my uniform cap. Before long, he would enter an advanced training corps to learn marksmanship in a faster plane. His lively air and bronzed face expressed tremendous masculine vigour. Impossible to imagine that, six months ago, he was to be found amongst the high school students, who generally held strong anti-militarist views. One would have taken him for a regular pilot of long experience. How could I account for this transformation? Was it due to the rather tense atmosphere of military life? His own will? He returned my salute and ran towards the barracks.

The new *tokusos* continued marching for a further two and a half miles or so past the airfield till we came to the entrance to some broken-down billets. Enclosed by an embankment planted with shrubs, they looked more like infantry huts; there was no sentry on duty and weeds had invaded the empty, abandoned shacks. No one would ever have suspected that this was a military camp. Evidently, there was no other habitation for miles around. It was as desolate as an uninhabited island far out in the ocean.

Led by the two cadets, the future airmen crossed the entrance and assembled in the courtyard between two lines of huts. A young officer climbed on to a bench and curtly announced: 'Attention! I am Flying Officer Ebara. I am going to take roll call. You will be divided into six squads. When you hear your name called, line up in front of the hut that bears a number corresponding to your squad. . . .'

Six N.C.O.'s were waiting for the new *tokusos*. The roll call proceeded.

'Fourth Squad,' said Flying Officer Ebara: 'Yukio Watanabe, Shogo Tsubouchi, Ryuji Nagatsuka, Mamoru Ishikawa . . .'

So, I was in the 4th Squad.

Suddenly, the weather broke and we heard thunder. A few minutes later, torrential rain began to fall. There are frequent storms in this region of Tochigui-Ken. Unruffled, the flying officer continued the roll call. We had to await permission to enter the huts. Everyone was drenched to the skin.

'That is all! I know you are impatient to go into your billets, but you are no longer students. As from tomorrow, you are officer cadets in the Air Fleet of the Imperial Army. Will the enemy hold up the battle just because it's raining? Right, dismiss!'

At the entrance to the quarters, an N.C.O. gave each man two uniforms, two military caps and a winter flying suit. But no Triplex goggles, no flying helmet and no 'summer suit', as the unlined flying suits were called.

'That's odd!' murmured Watanabe. 'After all, we're not foot-sloggers. Why don't they issue us with helmets and a summer suit?'

A flying officer came into the billets. He was not wearing a pilot's insignia either. He watched us putting on our uniforms for a moment, then shouted: 'Attention! You are soldiers now. The first man to see a superior officer come into the quarters must call out "Attention!" You will stop whatever you are doing and salute him in proper military fashion. I am Flying Officer Sakai, in charge of the Fourth Squad. This squad is divided into two flights. Those trainees whose names I call out belong to the first flight, the rest to the second. Cadet Pilots Takebuchi, Higaki, Watanabe, Nagatsuka, Tsubouchi . . .'

I was in the first flight. A flight consisted of twenty cadets, a squad of forty. In all, 240 new *tokusos* had just entered the camp at Kanamaruhara, an annex of the flying school at Utsunomiya.

'Right!' he went on. 'Assembly at eighteen hundred hours, in front of headquarters. Swords will be worn. Squadron Leader Minami, commanding officer of Kanamaruhara camp, will give you your orders. Carry on dressing!'

'Attention!' shouted a cadet loudly.

We saluted Flying Officer Sakai as he left the billets. We were now indeed soldiers. Weren't we addressed as 'Cadet Pilot Watanabe,' 'Cadet Pilot Nagatsuka,' etc? We looked at our-selves in uniform: we wore the pilots' insignia on our chests and the insignia of warrant officer and special cadet on our collars. To my amazement, we looked like a bunch of real officers. And only a moment ago we were students! Incredible , , ,

'At last,' said Cadet Pilot Watanabe, 'we are officer cadets in the Air Fleet of the Imperial Army. We must show ourselves worthy of the honour!'

Without knowing why, I felt drawn to this young man, who had been studying law at a private university in Tokyo, where he also went in for rowing. He was of medium height and build and, in spite of a calm and rather sweet expression, seemed energetic and daring. His uniform suited him.

Just as we were leaving the billets to assemble at head-quarters, a leading aircraftman stopped Watanabe and said to him: 'It seems to me, Cadet Pilot, that your cap is too far back.'

'Do you think so?' he asked.

He pushed his cap forward, then turned to me. 'Is that the right angle?' I nodded.

'Thank you,' he said to the leading aircraftman. 'I am Cadet Pilot Watanabe. What is your name?'

'Leading Aircraftman Kawasaki, Cadet Pilot,' replied the N.C.O., standing at attention.

Watanabe had first used the formal style of address, but had had the presence of mind to use the familiar style immediately afterwards. Although the N.C.O. was an experienced soldier and we were not, he was our junior in rank. Watanabe was therefore perfectly correct.

'Oh, Lord!' Watanabe said to me with a wry smile. 'It seems I can't get rid of that student habit of wearing my cap on the back of my head. Now that we're officers, we'll have to mend our ways, eh?'

At 1750 hours, the 240 new cadet pilots, lined up in full uniform, were awaiting Squadron Leader Minami in front of the headquarters building. The deluge had ceased; the sky was clear, glowing. Drops of water, caught in the foliage, sparkled in the rays of the setting sun like the ripples on a lake. The smell of brand-new uniforms, mingled with the effluvia of damp soil, gave us recruits a very real sensation of being soldiers.

Whispering was forbidden. What were my comrades thinking about in this absolute silence? The lushness of the vegetation reminded me of walks I had taken with my parents and sisters in a forest on the outskirts of Nagoya when I was a pupil at grammar school. I would never again know the pleasure of strolling with my family amongst verdant nature.

'Attention!' The order cut through my reverie. A superior

16

officer appeared on the steps. He seemed proud of the insignia he wore – that of the diploma of the Advanced School of Warfare. However, he was not wearing a pilot's badge. No, he could not be a pilot, for he wore glasses on his tapering nose. He ran his eye over the trainees before giving us a veritable lecture:

'Now that you have put on your uniforms and wear the pilot's insignia, you are members of the Imperial Army. You are no longer civilians, from whom much must be hidden. I am going to tell you the whole truth about the present state of the war. Italy's capitulation, on the fifth of September last year, has had a great influence on the war in the Pacific, insofar as it has restored Allied mastery of the sea and air in the Mediterranean, thus enabling the Allies to release their fleets to the Indian Ocean. Moreover, Badoglio's government has declared war on Germany. Attacked from both sides, Germany can no longer hope to conquer Great Britain. And our own country is compelled to fight the Allies single-handed in the Pacific. We are losing our battles. In the central Pacific Ocean, defeat follows upon defeat. The Tarawa atoll in the Gilbert Islands has been recaptured by the enemy after very heavy fighting. And so we have lost four thousand six hundred and ninety men – some amongst them took their own lives. Then there was the defeat of the atoll of Makin. The Twenty-seventh U.S. Division took four days to conquer this island, and the seven hundred and ninety-eight men in the garrison, commanded by Colonel Ichikawa, died heroically almost to the last man on the twenty-sixth of November. After the Gilbert Islands, the Americans attacked the Marshall Islands, contrary to all the predictions made by our navy. Even the Kwajalein atoll has been captured by the foe. This reconquest of the central Pacific, beginning with Tarawa, has isolated and wiped out our garrisons, one by one, depriving them of all supplies.

'To our great sorrow, our navy, which had already completely lost supremacy at sea, has allowed enemy submarines to invade the territorial waters of Japan. The *Konrin-Maru* was in fact sunk by an American submarine within Japanese waters in October.

'At the moment, it is essential to realise the seriousness of the check to Operation "Ro-Go", which was launched on the twenty-eighth of October. This plan aimed at the destruction of the enemy's naval air forces. Admiral Koga, commander-in-chief of the Combined Fleet, gave orders that the planes on board our aircraft carriers *Zuikaku, Zuiho* and *Shokaku*, of the first Naval Air Fleet, should be based at Rabaul.

'On the first of November, the Third Marine Division managed to land on Cape Torokina, in the island of Bougainville. This cape is situated two hundred and ninety-four miles from Rabaul. Admiral Koga therefore ordered the Second Naval Air Fleet, commanded by Admiral Takeo Kurita, to press on as far as Rabaul. On the fifth of November, when Admiral Koga's naval force reached Rabaul, they were attacked by ninety-seven bombers and fighters of the Thirty-eighth U.S. Task Force, the planes taking off from the aircraft carriers *Saratoga* and *Princeton*. In a second attack, the Thirty-eighth Task Force was supported by the Fifty-eighth and succeeded in knocking Admiral Koga's fleet out of combat. Four of our heavy cruisers, two light cruisers and five destroyers were more or less seriously damaged and one destroyer was sent to the bottom. As for our Naval Air Fleet based on Rabaul, we had a hundred and seventy-eight aircraft with seven hundred and twenty-eight men on board. Of these, a hundred and twenty-one aircraft were lost between the fifth and the seventeenth of November, forcing Admiral Koga to abandon Operation "Ro-Go" on the thirteenth of November. The loss of men and materials was very heavy, it cannot be denied . . .'

Squadron Leader Minami stopped to take a breath, for he had been speaking very rapidly. He stared at the new cadet pilots who were listening to him with tense faces.

Then he went on:

'Further, our Naval Air Fleet suffered great damage at Truk, which we called "the unsinkable aircraft carrier" and the Americans called "the Pacific Gibraltar". On the tenth of February, Admiral Koga ordered his fleet, composed of the flagship *Musashi*, the battleships *Nagato* and *Fuso* and the heavy cruisers *Atago, Chokai*, etc., to abandon Truk. He wanted to avoid a decisive engagement with the American fleet, for our navy would have been helpless without aircraft carriers and, at that time, they were all in Japan undergoing repairs after the arduous Battle of the Solomons. The Fourth Fleet, under the orders of Admiral Kobayashi, was entrusted with the defence of the island. Our air strength at Truk consisted of one hundred and forty-three planes, but one-half of these were not fit for service. There were also one hundred and thirty-five planes destined for transportation to the Southeast Pacific. In mid-February, enemy attacks having ceased, Admiral Kobayashi and his men relaxed their vigilance. But suddenly, at oh four hundred and fifty-five hours on the seventeenth of February, the first wave of seventy planes from the Fifty-eighth Task Force dived on Truk. Vice-Admiral Mitscher had given the order. Our aircraft, taken by surprise, were destroyed one after the other as Mitscher sent his planes in, four hundred and fifty of them in nine waves, right up until seventeen hundred hours. They circled over the base, machine-gunning and bombing the hangars without encountering any opposition. The field at Truk blazed all day long. As a result of this raid, we have only one fighter and five torpedo bombers left. Next day, Mitscher's force undertook the destruction of naval vessels at anchorage. Our transport ships were assembled in Truk, which was a relay base for the Southeast Pacific. Since we had no planes flying over the harbour, the enemy bombers were able to locate and destroy their targets undisturbed by any counter-attack; eyewitnesses say it was just as if the Americans were calmly carrying out exercises. And so Truk became the Japanese Pearl Harbor. Almost two hundred and seventy aircraft lost, nine warships and thirty-four transport ships sunk, nine warships severely damaged, and, on land, nearly six hundred men dead or wounded. Moreover, the convoy of the Fifty-second Division was attacked by the enemy about eighty miles west of Truk and there we lost two troop ships and twelve hundred men. That is the disastrous balance-sheet of two days' raids on Truk. And the Eniwetok atoll, deprived of reinforcements which should have been sent to them from Truk, was conquered on the twenty-fourth of February. In this way, the Americans have gained complete domination of the Marshall Islands. The small islands around Truk, rendered unusable in a miltary sense, are at present under enemy attack. Our own aircraft from Rabaul have been grouped for the defence of the island of Truk. Consequently there is at this moment only one single plane in Rabaul, in spite of the great strategic importance of that base . . . '

Squadron Leader Minami's eyes glittered with profound bitterness. Still standing rigidly at attention, I could not look at my comrades, but I sensed that they were biting their lips in rage, just as I was. The Americans' clear advantage in the central Pacific seemed to leave Japan with no hope of exploiting her early successes. And where was our Combined Fleet – reputedly invincible – at this moment?

The death of Admiral Koga, successor to Admiral Yamamoto, had been another shock for the Japanese nation. These distressing circumstances had forced the naval and military Chiefs of Staff to resign. They had been replaced by General Tojo and Admiral Shimada. From then on, Prime Minister Tojo held both the portfolio of the Minister of Armed Forces and the post of Chief of Imperial General Staff in the army. Hardly a wise move, since it is self-evident that the responsibility of the Prime Minister in the political sphere should not have been conjoined with the supreme command of the army.

Prime Minister Tojo was too much occupied by political problems to render a balanced judgement of military operations. Thus in May, the Military General Staff ordered the 15th Army to press on stubbornly with Operation Imphal [aimed at occupying the northeastern corner of India and so ensuring the defence of Burma] in spite of the problem of supplying the front line. This difficulty, which should have been foreseen, had brought the campaign to a standstill, and on May 15 General Hata reported to Tojo: 'The chances of Operation Imphal succeeding are growing fainter and fainter.' Nevertheless, the order was given: 'Take Imphal at all costs.' This was being absurdly optimistic, and if General Tojo had been less preoccupied he would surely have put the brake on the enthusiasm of his General Staff.

What would become of Japan? Was the outcome of the war now totally unpredictable? The loud voice of our commanding officer interrupted my thoughts:

'Now,' he concluded after a brief silence, 'you must view the present situation only in the light of what opportunities it offers our country. All our fighting men in the front lines are crying out for more planes and more pilots.

'Victory depends on mastery of the air. It is your task to regain it. As future pilots, you are thus assuming heavy responsibilities, and the training you are about to undergo will be all the more rigorous because of our urgent need for pilots. It may be that, a year from now, you will no longer be able to enjoy the sight of our beautiful countryside, but I hope that you will devote yourselves to your training and be ready to sacrifice your youth for your country. You will spend thirty days here. Before ending my talk, I wish to say only one word to you: Courage! Break ranks!'

A year from now, we new *tokusos* would no longer be able to enjoy the beauties of our countryside. The words just spoken by our commanding officer implied that within the course of the year every one of us must die in action. At that moment, we became fully aware of our destiny. Until now, we had avoided looking at its fatal consequences. We looked at one another. Now, it was an ineluctable reality, we must face it without flinching. And yet, at the bottom of our hearts, something denied this tragic inevitability. Each man said to himself that our leader's words could be interpreted as meaning that the cadet pilots would not be sent to the front for a year.

'How lovely nature is!' someone said. 'Since we shall not be alive to enjoy it much longer, let's steep ourselves in its charms.' Far from being a cry of despair, the voice expressed the serenity of the speaker's soul. It was as if he had always been prepared for death. Just as some of us were lifting our eyes to the rich green crowning the trees, an officer called out: 'On the double! Don't dawdle! Trainees must run at all times!'

With one accord, the cadet pilots began to run towards the quarters, our left hands holding our swords at our sides.

Back in the billets, members of the 4th Squad studied a notice posted on the wall. The dingy sleeping quarters, thick with dust, had no decoration other than this poster, which was a schedule of the thirty days' training programme:

06:00	Reveille
07:10	Study of military manuals; the mechanics of aircraft engines; meteorology
10:20–12:30	Flight training in gliders
13:10–18:00	Ditto
19:30	Study
21:30	Roll call
22:00	Curfew

What a disillusionment! Cadet Pilot Watanabe turned to me and said mournfully: 'Look at that! We're starting on gliders! Thirty long days to get through before they train us to fly planes. I hadn't expected that.'

That same morning, I had gone for a walk in my uncle's

garden with my parents, and we had watched an *Akatonbo* flying overhead. 'That's a training plane,' my father had said. 'Tomorrow, you'll be flying one of those. Are you pleased?' Nothing would have induced me to believe we would start by piloting gliders. No wonder Watanabe was disappointed. I nodded to him and was about to express my own surprise, when another cadet joined our conversation.

'Allow me to introduce myself, Cadet Pilot Takebuchi,' he said very solemnly. 'I belong to the Students' Flying Club and have ten hours' flying to my credit. As far as I know, flying a plane is entirely different from flying a glider. The handling of an aircraft is much more stable. I can't see how this glider training will help in learning to pilot a plane.'

'You may be right,' said Watanabe, 'but orders are orders, we can't dispute them.'

'Salute!' someone shouted.

He had just seen Flying Officer Sakai come in. We all stood at attention and saluted. Followed by an N.C.O., he ordered us to line up by our beds.

'At ease!' he called. 'I am going to give you some detailed information. Glider training starts tomorrow. This is Leading Aircraftman Kawasaki, who will be your instructor. His rank is lower than yours, which means he must salute you first. Nevertheless, you are to obey him without question in everything concerning your training. This will take place in a corner of the airfield at Kanamaruhara. It is two miles from the billets to the airfield. You will always cover this distance at a run. And remember, you are no longer civilians, you must get rid of your student attitudes. It is strictly forbidden to address your comrades formally. In the army, you will invariably use the forms *ore* and *kisama*.'*

For a whole hour, the new batch of trainees listened to instructions. No days off, no leave until the training was completed. Further, we were obliged to learn by heart the sacred words of the Emperor laying down the duties of a soldier and the rules which he must follow. This meant memorising some 27,000 words within the next three days. We were forbidden to speak to the women who worked in the kitchens. All

---

Ore is the familiar first person singular and *kisama* the familiar second person form. *Kisama* corresponds very roughly to *tu* in French, but it must be noted that in civilian life to use *kisama* in addressing non-intimates is insulting.

correspondence would be censored. To our astonishment, we would have to carry out sentry duty at night and kitchen fatigues by day, which meant distributing meals and washing the mess tins. Theoretically, officers did not have to carry out these tasks, which were the lot of the rank and file. However, according to Flying Officer Sakai, the *tokusos* would be treated as ordinary troops for thirty days. When Sakai had left the room, Takebuchi said jokingly: 'A cadet pilot with a sword at his side and a mess tin in his hand is a pretty sight. He wouldn't dare show himself to his fiancée, who no doubt imagines him looking like a dashing young pilot, elegant and martial!'

There was a roar of laughter. But we had no time to lose: before dinner, we had to clean out the dusty billets from top to bottom. These shacks had long been abandoned and the floor, of beaten earth, was bristling with weeds. There were other chores to be done: sewing the cadet pilots' insignia on to our uniforms and battle dress, making a bundle of our student clothing, etc.

It was 2030 when the trainees sat down to table in the dimly lit room. Flying Officers Sakai and Ebara sat at the same table with us. Unlike Sakai, who was always very serious, Flying Officer Ebara was rubicund and smiling. He was the officer attached to the 4th Squad.

Our appetites were roused by the sight of a generous slice of meat, a whole grilled sea bream and a bowl of *sekihan* [rice cooked with red beans]. It is the custom in Japan to eat these last two dishes when celebrating a happy event. Such a meal would have been hard to find now in civilian life.

'Well, well,' said Ebara with cool irony, 'this is an excellent meal. It is to celebrate the first day of your military service. You may rest assured that you will be well fed, but do not imagine you will get as good as this every day. The army treats all its soldiers in the same way. It is a fact that, as pilots, you will be constantly exposed to the risk of death, even during training, but do not abuse your special and privileged position.'

Behind these words there was a gleam of jealousy towards the budding pilots who had jumped to the rank of warrant officer without the slightest military experience. He had spent eighteen months training to become an officer, like men in the reserve. Furthermore, he and Flying Officer Sakai were non-flying personnel, members of the Aviation Service Corps.

'By the way,' he went on, 'speed is an essential ingredient in the life of a serving man. From tomorrow, you must eat your meals in a quarter of an hour. Never forget that training takes absolute priority.'

During dinner, he gave out the rota for night guard duty and kitchen fatigue up to the 30th of June. Watanabe was on guard duty that very first night.

'You (*Kimi*) are out of luck!' murmured Takebuchi, nudging Watanabe.

Ebara's smiling face turned into a scowling mask; he had overheard Takebuchi's words.

'So you still can't get rid of your student habits!' he observed sourly. 'I told you, no formal style of address!'

After dinner, there was roll call, and shortly after that the bugler sounded curfew. A melancholy sound! It is said to evoke sad and morbid thoughts in all new recruits. But for us, the young and eager cadet pilots, it was different. The bugle sang gaily that training would begin next day.

Lying in bed, I passed my hand over the *sen-nin bari* tied round my waist. *Sen-nin bari* means literally 'a thousand stitches worked by a thousand people.' It was a strip of silk on which a thousand women embroidered a little stitch. Only the fair sex had the right to make it, just as only they could ask passers by in the street to add a stitch. During the war, it was a common sight to see women stitching the *sen-nin bari* at the request of other women. It was a sort of talisman superstitiously believed to be as effective as a bullet-proof vest. Mothers and wives gave them to their menfolk off to the wars. Japanese soldiers always wore them, knotted around their waists.

My mother's great love for me emanated from this piece of stuff. I saw her again, bowing to passers by in the streets of Nagoya and begging them to add a stitch. She had had only three days to finish the *sen-nin bari*. During those three days, she must have been tormented by unutterable anguish, but she hid it behind a proud and smiling mask, so that no one would have guessed at her suffering. What was she doing now, at this moment? Was she in my uncle's house at Koga, talking to my father?

There was nothing to be heard now but the muffled footsteps of Watanabe, who was mounting guard. The absolute calm of night lulled the trainees to sleep. Already I could hear the regular breathing of those who were asleep. The first day of our military service was melting into oblivion, carrying with it a thousand varied emotions.

I too slipped imperceptibly into sleep.

Next day, a new life began.

At six o'clock, reveille sounded in all four corners of the camp. We had only five minutes to make our beds, put on our uniforms, and present ourselves on parade in the courtyard. After muster, we hastily brushed our teeth and swallowed breakfast before attending the course at 7 a.m. In the army, the appointed hour means the hour at which one must be in action; it was therefore essential to be ready five minutes beforehand.

In the evening, as soon as we returned to barracks, we rushed to get through a mountain of chores: polishing shoes, washing clothes, burnishing swords and so on. Happily, we did not have rifles. A soldier spent a long time cleaning his rifle and was also bound to wash the underwear of N.C.O.'s and veterans. A cadet's life is heaven on earth compared to that of a soldier, who was perpetually supervised by the N.C.O.'s. We were never struck in the face. The pitiful life of a recruit, as it had been described to me, was unthinkable here.

Even so, the trainees found washing clothes a very tiresome task. As students, not one of us had ever had to do it before. A pilot must always wear clean clothing, as he risks his life each time he flies, and a dirty shirt would bring disgrace upon a pilot who was accidentally killed. Like a Samurai, he must be cleanly dressed at all times. Moreover, there were frequent kit inspections without warning. And very strict they were too – one dirty sock and you were punished. It became a joke with some of us: 'We're such good laundresses, we won't need to get married!'

After putting our kit in order, we bathed and dined rapidly before study hour. The flying officer had been right when he stressed that the first day's meal was not typical. The meals that followed were much less generous: a bowl of rice mixed with maize and a few vegetables and garnished with a tiny morsel of meat. The food situation in Japan had reached the crisis point. The cadets, worn out by the training programme, had appetites like wolves. Hunger is a kind of hell, and the only way we could assuage it was to dream of a world of

25

plenty, for, oddly enough, when we imagined ourselves eating to our hearts' content, we actually felt sated. Watanabe could do a perfect imitation of a cook preparing *sushi*, a typical rice dish served with a prawn, or other shellfish, on top. When our hunger became unbearable, we would say to him in fun: 'Waiter! Some *sushi* please!' Then Watanabe would amuse himself by asking: 'Would you prefer tuna fish or prawns, sir?' And while the rest of us watched with watering mouths, admiring his skill as a mime, he would set to imitating the cook. Perhaps this childish tomfoolery seems unworthy of officers of the Imperial Army, but at least it allowed us to get through a moment when we were dying of emptiness.

Watanabe had the kind of face that inspires sympathy and trust, and we soon became close friends.

The cadet pilots devoted their study hours to learning by heart the manuals on aerial tactics, the duties of an officer, the military code, and above all the sacred words of the Emperor, addressed to soldiers in the Imperial Army:

' . . . the serving man takes on a duty to serve his sovereign loyally. All citizens born in this country must be of one resolve: to devote themselves to their homeland. A soldier who is not filled with this resolve should not enlist, for no matter how erudite and skilled he may be in the military arts, a soldier who lacks the unshakable will to fulfil all his obligations to his country, must be considered as a good-for-nothing. A well-trained army, faithful to its rules of conduct, but lacking a spirit of boundless devotion and patriotism, would be little better than a disorderly rabble if put to the test . . . '

These sacred words were written in such a high-flown style that the soldiers had the greatest difficulty understanding them. But all army officers were compelled to learn them by heart. Years and years have passed, yet I can still recite the whole thing.

During the early days, we made desperate efforts to learn not only the Emperor's words but also the flight manuals and military regulations. Little light filtered in through the opaque windows of our billets so, as soon as we had a free moment, we would go outside. Even in the latrines, one could hear cadets reciting the words.

Above all, we were enamoured of the glider training. It took place every day, regardless of the weather, under the direction of Leading Aircraftman Kawasaki, who knew his job and was always calm and kindly. Even when it was pouring rain, you could hear the shouts of cadets as they pulled on the springs of the catapults.

In spite of the difference in rank, we had considerable respect for Kawasaki. Politely, and in detail, he would tell each pilot of his faults. We listened to him, in some embarrassment, since it was forbidden to speak to him individually in barracks because he was beneath us in rank. We knew nothing of his age or past history. Sometimes, there was a hint of melancholy in his expression. It was assumed that he had been among the *shonen hikohei* – boys of fourteen to sixteen recruited for training as pilots – but that, for some reason, he had been assigned to the Service Corps. Small and still young, he never behaved like the other N.C.O.'s, who were generally fierce, ruthless and diabolical.

We trainees always ran from the billets to the training field, singing battle songs as we went. We even ran to recover the gliders after landing, so as to gain more time for actual flying. During the one break of fifteen minutes allowed during the afternoon, we flopped down on the grass like huge tunny-fish stranded on the beach, some flat on their stomachs, others on their backs, fighting to regain our breath and quieten our pounding hearts. In the bright sunlight, those who hid their faces amongst the riotous weeds enjoyed the fleeting sensation of being alone and free. Others profited by this moment of leisure to recite the army regulations. The odour of damp soil and dry grass made us conscious that we were still alive, and set us wondering how much longer we would be able to enjoy the good, earthy smells. Who will ever know what passed through all our minds, as we gazed at the grass or at the blue sky dotted with trainers?

What is certain is that we missed our families and our student life. The leaders of each squad told us on every possible occasion to forget our memories, our longings and regrets, but they could not forbid us to recall our family life with joy, for no matter what people say, the family is still the basic unit of human life. It nourishes us, not only with bread, but with ideas, beliefs, sentiments and sensibilities. And it is the privilege of the past to be gilded and embellished as we look back on it.

Gradually, beginning by slithering along the ground, we young pilots became accustomed to flying gliders. A fortnight later, we could fly at a height of fifteen to twenty feet.

Our instructor Kawasaki was amazed at such progress. As soon as we had mastered the gliders, we would be allowed to pilot airplanes, even if it were before the scheduled date. This hope was our great incentive. We had steady nerves, since almost all of us had been athletes at university. There had not been a single accident since training began!

On the day when I first flew three feet off the ground, I had the vague impression that the sky held my fate in its hands. Unlike the earth, which supports us firmly, the sky rests on nothing. In this blank space, I had felt rather insecure and had instinctively pushed the stick into the landing position too early. However, at six feet . . . nine feet . . . twelve feet . . . as I gained altitude little by little each day, so I gained, little by little, the art of controlling the machine. At the start, I developed a tic: at the moment of take-off, I unconsciously kicked out with my right foot, which inevitably caused a rotation to the right. It occurred to me to adjust the rudder bar slightly towards the left to compensate for this. During the descent, just before landing, it was only necessary to press the stick very lightly. The glider eased down on its trajectory all by itself. The important thing was not to resist the currents of air, to use them, indeed, according to the elementary laws of aerodynamics.

Cadet pilots did not have time to read the newspapers or listen to the radio, which was in any case forbidden. Flying Officer Sakai, the leader of our squad, explained the progress of the war to us as it was set out in secret reports. I took detailed notes.

The Naval General Staff had drawn up Plan 'A-Go' on May 3. The aim of this operation was to annihilate the American Fleet by means of a concerted attack by the Combined Fleet commanded by Admiral Toyoda, successor to Admiral Koga, and to prevent an enemy counter offensive. On May 19, Admiral Ozawa, commander-in-chief of the 1st Mobile Fleet, had assembled his armada in the roadsteads of Tawitawi to the south of the Philippines: nine aircraft carriers, seven battleships, eleven heavy and three light cruisers, thirty-two destroyers. A total of seventy-three vessels, including eleven supply ships. There were 450 planes aboard the carriers. Besides this, the 1st Naval Air Fleet, commanded by Admiral Kakuta and composed of 1,664 planes, was deployed throughout the central Pacific and the Australian zone to await zero hour. The General Staff definitely anticipated that the enemy would establish his line of counterattack between New Guinea and Australia, and would take up our challenge in the Palau Islands. However, it was not difficult to predict that in fact the Americans would establish their counter offensive in the Marshall Islands and then try to take the Marianas. It was only 1,125 miles from Tokyo to Saipan. It did not take much imagination to realise that the enemy would want a base for his Task Force that would allow him to raid the Japanese mainland with the minimum difficulty. Nevertheless, our General Staff attached little importance to a possible U.S. attack on the Marianas. 'Our army is now deploying a considerable force to ensure the defence of the Marianas,' they said. 'After the disembarkation of the Forty-third Division, which is expected to take place in mid-May, we are certain that we can repulse an invasion of these islands.' Furthermore, General Tojo declared flatly that Saipan was impregnable.

Saipan was in the heart of the Marianas: one and a half to five and a half miles wide by twelve miles in length. It was not an atoll, like Tarawa and Makin, but a real island, dominated by Mount Tapotchau, 1,540 feet high. The two largest towns, Garapen and Charankanoa, were on the western seacoast. Sugar-refining, fishing and stock-breeding were highly developed industries in Garapen, while Charankanoa boasted two large factories. The island also possessed an excellent air base in the south. It was impossible to overlook its economic and strategic importance. The Central Pacific Fleet, under the command of Admiral Nagumo, and the 31st Army were entrusted with its defence: more than 30,000 men in all. General Yoshitsugu Saito, commanding officer of the 43rd Division, had arrived there at the end of May.

On May 27, the Americans had landed on Biak Island, just off the north coast of New Guinea. This attack had persuaded our General Staff that the next American strike would be directed against the New Guinea–Philippines axis. The navy was keeping its eyes riveted to the Palau Islands with the intention of mounting a great naval battle against the U.S. Fleet. This had been the dream of all the commanders-in-chief of our Combined Fleet, from Admiral Yamamoto on.

However, our army was suddenly placed in a critical and unforeseen position: on June 11, Admiral Mitscher, commander of the 58th Task Force, launched his fighters from eight aircraft carriers and raided the Marianas: Rota, Guam, Saipan and Tinian. Our General Staff were undecided as to whether this was the signal for a decisive onslaught on the Marianas or an isolated attack of little importance. After examining the situation, it was deemed that the enemy would not be capable of mounting a large-scale operation against the Marianas before November. In spite of a second raid the following day, it was still believed that the Americans' number-one objective was the Paulau Islands. Admiral Ozawa alone did not share this opinion. On June 13, he ordered his fleet to raise anchor and sail into waters west of Saipan; he was convinced his ships would confront the enemy in this zone.

The Palaus or the Marianas? Which was the enemy's real objective? The cadet pilots were divided on this point. 'Of course,' declared Takebuchi, 'it's bound to be the Palaus. But on the sixth of June, the Allies landed on the coast of Normandy in France. This important operation in Europe will delay action in the Pacific.'

'No!' answered Watanabe. 'The Marianas constitute the first true line of defence of our country. Indeed, Saipan is strictly within Japanese territory, and its conquest would be a tremendous advance for the enemy. In my opinion, the Americans will attempt a landing on Saipan.'

'Alas!' said Takebuchi. 'We haven't sufficient strength to defend Saipan. If the Americans do try a landing there, it will be very serious.'

'Yes. And don't forget the Americans have just put a gigantic bomber into service – the B-29. They say it can carry four tons of bombs and has a range of thirty-five hundred miles. Now, the distance between Tokyo and Saipan is not even half the range of a B-29. With this plane, direct flights from Saipan to Tokyo become perfectly feasible, so the conquest of Saipan would bring the Japanese archipelago within the reach of air raids. Obviously the Americans intend to try for a landing there.'

The cadet pilots discussed the enemy's plans with passionate intensity. 'It is not for you to discuss these matters,' Sakai said to us. 'It is enough that you devote yourselves assiduously to your training.'

In spite of this exhortation, no one could remain unconcerned. If the unthinkable happened, and Saipan fell into

American hands, Japan, and consequently our own families, would be exposed to the greatest dangers. Without admitting it, we felt a presentiment that it would be our eventual destiny to fight the B-29.

June 18. I was on sentry duty. The moon stood out against a pitch-black sky. I made the rounds of our huts. There was not a sound but the erratic rustling of the wind through the foliage. The darkness, the absence of human sound, lent a sinister air to our camp. I had the uncanny feeling that the wretched appearance of our shacks symbolised our country's tragic fate. It was undeniable that our chances of victory had drastically diminished. 'A will of iron can accomplish anything': that was what the high command kept repeating ad nauseam. According to them, a bamboo cane, filled with the traditional fighting spirit of Japan, was sufficient to overcome an adversary armed to the teeth. But could we really believe in this fanatical mysticism? It is related that in the thirteenth century a sudden and providential tempest repulsed the Mongol invaders, led by Kubla Khan, by sending all their ships to the bottom off the coast of Kyushu. This was cited as an instance of the divine protection exercised at all times in favour of our country. We were proud of it. 'The Japanese Empire is sacred and inviolable. Any American pilot who dares to invade our air space will inevitably be the object of divine vengeance,' a journalist had written. A bizarre idea, but some people believed it in good faith. But nothing was more absurd than to wait, with arms folded, for this kind of divine intervention. The situation of our land forces was desperate: there was no longer any miracle that could save them. New means to redress the military balance of power had to be found. But . . . what means? My mind came up against a blank wall.

Whenever I was alone, this anxiety gnawed at me, although I normally shared my comrades' enthusiasm. I stood still and raised my eyes to heaven to chase away these morbid thoughts. Above me, countless stars shone. Spending the night in the open, I had the obscure feeling that, while the cadets slept, a mysterious world awoke. The stars in their eternal solitude affected a total indifference to the interminable conflicts of mankind. More than that, one would almost have said they were laughing amongst themselves, jeering derisively far above this lowly world where men gave free rein to their belligerent

31

instincts. Just as I was about to resume my rounds, I noticed that the headquarters building, normally dark at this hour, was lit up, bathed in a strange illumination. From a distance, I could make out hurrying figures. What was going on? I looked at my watch by the glimmer of the moon; it was three o'clock. A soldier ran up to me, saluted and said: 'Cadet pilot, emergency muster! In full uniform!'

'Right! Thank you . . . '

The words were not out of my mouth before a blast on the bugle shattered the silence of night. This gay bugle call was like the buzzing of a disturbed beehive; it shook the barracks. Each bugle call had its special character: reveille was an animated crescendo designed to arouse the fighting spirit; lights-out was a descrescendo that evoked melancholy.

I rushed into the huts shouting: 'In full uniform!'

Then I went to change my clothes.

'Full field dress?' asked Cadet Pilot Ishikawa in a sleepy voice. 'Then it must be leave. They're going to tell us we've got forty-eight hours' leave. What a bit of luck!'

He was always pining for his family, and did not hide it. We laughed at his unwonted optimism, which was totally out of place. Nobody bothered to answer him.

Squadron Leader Minami was waiting for us in front of headquarters. His face was closed and tense. Everyone had been summoned with the exception of the N.C.O.'s and troopers. The commanding officer began to speak; his clear, ringing voice resounded in the darkness:

'Saipan has become the hot spot in the Pacific,' he said. 'At eighteen forty-nine hours on the fifteenth of June, the U.S. Marines finally succeeded in establishing a beachhead at Charankanoa, after fighting since early morning. The day before yesterday, at oh-thirty-eight hours, forty-seven B-29 bombers took off from a base in China and raided Yahata, in northern Kyushu. The iron and steel works were not too badly damaged. The enemy lost only seven aircraft. For the first time since the Doolittle raid, the sky over our country has been violated. That is a fact.'

His voice quivered with exasperation and a profoundly felt anger.

'The east coast of Saipan is bounded by cliffs,' the squadron leader went on. 'It was evident, therefore, that the Americans would try to land on the west coast. General Saito had laid down his line of defence according to the plan drawn up by General Obata, commander-in-chief of the Thirty-first Army, which aimed at wiping out the enemy on the seashore. Taking into account the nature of the terrain, it would have been better to establish defensive positions in the mountains. As it was, our men, for lack of equipment, had to make do with digging themselves holes in the sand, as their only means of shelter. Moreover, the enemy was master of the air over Saipan. Our First Naval Air Fleet, having suffered heavy losses in men and planes, was virtually impotent. Malaria had also worked its ravages. There remained no more than thirty or forty aircraft in the Saipan zone. General Saito had another problem: the twenty-five thousand civilians who lived on the island were hampering the movement of our troops.

'At oh-eight forty-three the first wave of assault troops, in amphibious vehicles, hit the beaches, and by oh-nine hundred hours four battalions, that is to say, eight thousand men, were massed on the beaches of Charankanoa. There were more than one thousand dead and wounded. Caught in the ferocious fire from our big guns, mortars and machine guns placed on the heights, the U.S. Marines had to dig shelters using hands and helmets as their only tools. In these improvised trenches, American army surgeons amputated arms and legs without even taking the time to anaesthetise the victims.

'From sixteen hundred to oh-three hundred hours, one of our battalions carried out the first counterattack against the left flank of the enemy beachhead. They caused great confusion amongst the enemy, who had lost their commanding officer. But before long the battleship *California* fired a salvo of artillery fire against our troops. The precision of their aim was facilitated by the discharge of tracer shells from three destroyers standing in close to the shore. We were forced to fall back on Garapan. In the early hours, almost seven hundred Japanese dead were found at the bridgehead. This counter-attack had not even succeeded in penetrating the first American lines.

'To sum up,' concluded Minami, 'the sacred Japanese archipelago now lies under the threat of American bombardment. The responsibility rests still more heavily upon our pilots. I hope this will inspire you to apply yourselves even more diligently to your training.'

Several of the cadets, without admitting it, had been almost

3

ready to believe in the hope of leave. The commanding officer's harangue had completely wiped out their secret hopes. This was hardly the moment for leave!

Back in our quarters, we slipped hastily into our beds, without a word, racked with anxiety and painful emotions. The silence weighed heavily.

From that day on, the trainees found that time dragged by with unbearable slowness. We were dying to pilot real airplanes instead of gliders.

One day, I received a letter from my old teacher, who had been drafted into war work. 'We lead a rather inactive life in the factory I hope with all my heart that you and your class-mates will soon have the opportunity to resume your studies, and I hope that the arduous life of the army has not made you forget all your French. Do you remember the French for egg plant, and cucumber?'

I had not yet written to him, nor had I written to my family or my high school friends. Why not? In the first place, because our day was packed too full, there was no time. Secondly, the censorship inhibited me from expressing myself freely. I did not want to write banalities: 'I am very well . . . ' 'I am making every effort to become a first-class pilot . . . ' 'I will fight like a tiger to defend our country . . . ' etc. Although I was not being tormented by the N.C.O.'s, there were many things I would have liked to write about the absurdity of the army. For example, our instructors insisted that the essential thing was to capture the spirit of the Emperor's sacred words, and, to this end, we were compelled to learn them by heart. But the quarters were very poorly lit, so reading under these circumstances would inevitably ruin our eyesight, and if there is one thing that is absolutely indispensable to a pilot it is good eyesight! Our Service Corps officers, including Flying Officer Ebara, never took this into account. Ebara, in particular, openly indulged in petty jealousies. I would have liked to write to Professor Arinaga about these things.

After reading this letter, I stretched out on my bed and began to sing *Sous les Toits de Paris*:

> *Quand elle eut vingt ans,*
> *Sa vieille maman lui dit un jour tendrement . . .*

I had learned the song from a French film.
Someone tapped my shoulder. It was Watanabe.

'Ah!' he said, 'how that song takes me back . . .'

'You mean I am still dreaming of my student days?'

'Between ourselves, so am I,' he confessed. 'I don't claim to be an intellectual, like you. I barely paid attention to the lectures, I was much keener on sports. Even if I had taken a degree at my university, I should only have become a humble bank clerk, or something like that. So the only thing for me is to do my damnedest at this moment. Well, I've tried hard, but I still don't feel I've got into the skin of an officer. I am well aware of my failings, but what can I do? We were only called up three weeks ago, that's not very long. Anyway, it's no use moaning!'

He was a decent man. He never gave way to weakness in such difficult moments. Yet his confession revealed to me that he too suffered from the harshness of reality, in spite of the serene air he affected.

And as for me? I must admit, I still nursed my nostalgia for French literature which I had hoped to study at University. Nostalgia at times turned to discontent with my present lot, and fear that the dream of becoming a keen and erudite scholar would be dashed to the ground. I kept telling myself, over and over again, that I must prepare myself simply to face death, even though a vague and far-off hope of escaping my fate persisted in the deepest recesses of my mind.

But how did my family and my companions see me? No doubt, as an impeccable officer. There was an ambiguity in this which made me feel ashamed. And so I had another enemy to fight, besides the Americans: the contradictions within myself. It was intolerable and plunged me into profound distress.

It was already the rainy season. Gentle rain fell every day. The steady, monotonous dripping from the edge of the gutterless roofs got on our nerves, especially in the evenings, when we were shut up in the gloomy and funereal atmosphere of the billets, which evoked something of the wretchedness in Gorki's *Lower Depths*, and was really painful to endure. How we envied our seniors, flying over our heads in *Akatonbos*!

At the end of the month, we would quit these uncomfortable hovels forever. And we would have no regrets! The day of departure drew near. Half the 240 cadet pilots would be assigned to the barracks in Kanamaruhara and the rest to the airfield at Mibu, some eight miles south of Utsunomiya. It was there that we would learn to fly airplanes.

On the eve of departure, each cadet was given a ration of *saké*. Curfew was deferred until midnight. We took advantage of this to hold a banquet, to which Flying Officers Sakai and Ebara were invited. Delighted to be leaving this hole, we amused ourselves with an impromptu talent show. Cadet Pilot Kadowaki, who had a very fine voice, sang 'The Song of My Native Land':

> Those mountains where I hunted hares,
> The stream I fished for little carp,
> Days full of sweetness slipped by uncounted,
> Ah! How can I forget my native land?

An old lament we had known since childhood. With lowered eyes, we listened, and our hearts melted. Perhaps we were all thinking of our families. It was natural enough. And was it not more human to express one's nostalgia openly, instead of repeating boastfully: 'It is our duty to sacrifice our lives for our country without the slightest regret?' I would have liked to reply: 'Is that honestly a true expression of the feelings in your heart?' It seemed I could never overcome my instinctive revolt against militarism.

In his turn, Watanabe sang a popular and rather bawdy song. He was a little drunk, and no doubt he wanted to dispel the melancholy evoked by the previous song. When he finished singing, he nudged me as if to say: 'It's your turn.'

But I was not in the mood to join in the spirit of the thing. Not that I bore the slightest ill-will towards my fellows. They had always shown themselves to be good-natured and calm, with the exception of Ishikawa, whom I did not like. Was I jealous? Was my critical mind pedantic, after all? I felt nothing but disgust for myself, and that is the truth of the matter.

By chance, my eyes met Sakai's. His eyes were smiling. I would have liked to open my heart to him, but it was impossible – he was my senior in rank! I bowed my head.

Next day, July first, there were few clouds in the sky in spite of the fact that we were in the rainy season. Cadets from the 2nd, 4th and 6th Squads were to leave for Mibu at eight o'clock. While I was folding up my jacket and uniform, to hand them in, Watanabe spoke to me:

'That's lucky! I'm glad we shall be together at Mibu.'

I agreed with him. I could always speak to him frankly.

Lined up on either side of a path that led to our door, other trainees were waiting for us. They were to be billeted in the barracks at Kanamaruhara. At eight o'clock, in full-dress uniform, we began to quick-march, led by Flying Officer Sakai. Our comrades saluted us and silently watched us go. In the navy, they would have waved their caps. There was no sound except the rhythm of our rapid steps. Would we ever have the pleasure of seeing them again? Perhaps not! For a moment, I gave way to sentimental reflections.

We followed the service path bordered with bushy trees, the same path we had trotted along between the airfield and the quarters. This time, we walked. The familiar landscape seemed different today. 'Not a single plane in sight, eh?' someone observed. Having finished their elementary training, the *tokusos* of the second intake must have left the Kanamaruhara field to make room for the third.

We travelled by train. Like animals who see men for the first time, we gazed curiously at the civilians in white shirts. It was thirty days since we had come in on this same train – but those thirty days seemed like ten years.

Towards midday, large patches of blue appeared in the cloudy sky. It was as if the sun was bidding us welcome. At the entrance to the barracks, there was a notice board, 'Training Corps of the Flying School of Utsunomiya at Mibu.' A sentry presented arms as the cadet pilots approached and, the moment we crossed the threshold, all the guards rose smartly from their benches. A bodyguard is a good indication of the standard of discipline in a regiment. We were all certain that an iron discipline reigned over this school – the kind that is the backbone of armies! Here was an authentic military atmosphere, as different from Kanamaruhara barracks as day is from night. On the vast expanse of the airfield, three fighter planes glinted in the sun. The barracks was an imposing building of two storeys. A duty officer, wearing a red and white riband from his right shoulder to his left hip, was waiting for the trainees on the square. He was a flying officer, and a pilot! His insignia was proudly displayed on his chest. He looked every inch the warrior-pilot: tall, broad-shouldered, of an iron constitution, and with piercing eagles' eyes in a handsome, serious face. He said curtly in a stentorian voice: 'Strip off completely! Soak your underwear and your uniforms in baths full of disinfectant!'

We gaped at one another. He spoke very distinctly, with a Kyushu accent. Far from being comical, this formal manner, this voice solemn as the grave, impressed us all.

'From now on,' he added, 'it is strictly forbidden to wear your *sen-nin baris* round your waists. They are nothing but a nest for lice. We aviators loathe lice above all things, though they are the friends and companions of the foot-sloggers.'

Ah, so that was the explanation! The flying school were afraid we might have brought in lice from our squalid ex-infantry quarters. We did not have fleas, but we brought in at least a few bugs. It was said that the underwear and *sen-nin bari* of an infantry soldier were crawling with lice, and you could see a black, squirming line in every fold. It was important that a pilot should never be bitten by these filthy vermin; during flight, the least itching could be a distraction and a danger.

After the disinfecting, we were subdivided into four squads, each comprising thirty cadets. I belonged to the first and was pleased to find Watanabe in my group. New uniforms were issued.

In the billets, we awaited the arrival of our leader with some curiosity. Vastly different from Kanamaruhara, the sleeping quarters were very bright: the floor, bedheads, windows, blankets and sheets were all clean and pleasing to the eye. The veteran *tokusos* had cleaned them the previous evening, before leaving for the advanced flying course. We were touched by the kindly consideration of these comrades, who were destined to die in battle before us. There was no doubt that they had wanted this order and cleanliness to convey to us their proud and heroic resolve to fight to the end. It was a kind of symbol.

The duty officer, followed by several other flying officers and cadets, came into our billets. His name was Flying Officer Komorizono and he was in charge of the 1st Squad. Other officers, veterans of the first intake of *tokusos*, were responsible for our training as pilots. We felt a certain fellow-feeling with them and, to judge from their friendly attitude, this was reciprocated. They gave out flying manuals, a flight card and meteorological maps. In the evening, they explained to us how to fill in the flight card and make use of the maps.

Flying Officer Komorizono, in spite of his brisk and dynamic appearance, was not a regular soldier. He held a diploma in physical culture from the Teachers' Training College. He was

proud of being a master of *kendo*, a military art widely prac-
tised in Japan. It is a kind of fencing and there are eight grades,
beginning with the first *dan*. Komorizono was a fourth *dan*.
Since he held a teacher's diploma, he was able to join up in the
kanbu-kohosei course where, as future officers, cadets studied
for a year at one of the special military schools and became
officers after six months' service. Then he had left the infantry
to become a pilot. This was also the case with the leader of the
3rd Squad, Flying Officer Hayashi. The leaders of the 2nd and
4th Squads, Flight Lieutenants Fukushima and Yamamoto,
were regular soldiers. They had all trained at the Army Flying
School, as had the commander-in-chief of the training corps at
Mibu, Squadron Leader Watanabe.

Senior cadet pilots showed us the various rooms: smoking
room, study, lecture room, mess, bathroom. Smoking was prohibited except in the smoking room. To our delight, we would
have no more kitchen fatigue and no more night guard duty.
And we no longer had to study the soldier's manual or the army
regulations. Our time would be devoted exclusively to learning
to fly.

Two squads took their flight training in the morning, the
two others in the afternoon, changing shifts every week. Apart
from the flying lessons, we had lectures on radio communica-
tions, meteorology and navigation. One free day per month.
No leave for a certain period. One of the greatest hazards for a
pilot was the slackening off he was liable to suffer after a period
of leave.

Training began next day. Reveille at 0430 hours to get the
trainers out of the hangars before morning parade. This allowed
us to set to work sharp at seven, immediately after breakfast.
Not one of us turned out with a sleepy face – we were all at
the peak of condition and eager to take our first steps in the
air, if I can so express it. Flying helmet and summer suit – we
looked at one another with satisfaction. The summer suit, made
of dark brown silk, was pleasing to the touch. It was this that
really gave us the feeling of being veritable pilots, at last.

While we were running towards the awning set up in the
middle of the airfield, our instructors were taxiing the
Akatonbos into position and lining them up on the tarmac. We
were excited by the rhythmic throbbing of the engines.

The first day: initiation flight. Luckily, the weather held fair.
The sun's rays, piercing the clouds from time to time, made the

black engine cowling glitter. Some small wild flowers, whose name I did not know, struck me as extraordinarily beautiful. I picked one and put it into the pocket of my summer suit. Perhaps I was instinctively following the tradition of the ancient Samurais who went into battle with a flower in their helmets. It helped me to retain my sensibility throughout the training, which became more and more gruelling. And was it not also my duty to protect the plants that grew in the soil of my native land? We sat down under the canvas awning and shortly afterwards Komorizono appeared.

'At last,' he said, 'you are to take your first steps as pilots. I have very little to say to you. In the army, it is only cowards and idlers who are forever asking "Why?" Nevertheless, and especially when you are at the controls of a plane, you will have to ask "Why and how?" At such times, think of nothing but piloting the plane. That is all.'

Each squad split up into six crews of five cadets each. Kagawa and Yamada were in my crew, together with Watanabe. Yamada had been a student at a private university in Kyoto, and spoke with the accent of that city. As he was cheerful and frankly naïve, some of the men delighted in teasing him, or even jeering at him, but he never lost his temper. Kagawa's temperament was just the opposite: he never spoke without weighing his words carefully beforehand, and was very serious. In spite of his short stature, he had been a member of the football team at the Commercial High School in Tobe. The instructor for our crew was Flight Sergeant Furuya.

The trainers began to take off one after the other. The *Akatonbo*, or Dragonfly, painted deep yellow with red circles on wings and fuselage, was a 480-horsepower biplane. Its theoretical ceiling was around 19,000 feet; its cruising speed, 150 miles per hour. Its official name was 'Training Airplane Model 95, Mark.' [Towards the end of the war, due to the desperate shortage of planes, it was used for special suicide-missions. Editor.]

It was my turn to fly after Yamada. At the moment of take-off, it came to me that this first step in the air was leading me to my death. As the plane gained altitude, houses, trees, roads dwindled, growing smaller and smaller – just so would my life slip away from me, day by day. Altitude: 3,900 feet. I had no sensation of flying, it was rather as if I were floating in the air, and it was not until the moment when I pierced the clouds that I had any sensation of speed. Would I glimpse my beloved Mount Fuji? I searched for it. No, visibility was not good enough. Suddenly, Furuya kicked me on the left leg. I turned round and he pointed to the left side of his head. Damn! I had completely forgotten to fasten the speaking tube to the mouthpiece of my 'intercom'. In spite of the care with which I had prepared for the flight, I had slipped up even before take-off! Fixing the intercom, I heard Furuya: 'Is your seat belt securely fastened? We're going to do some aerobatics. Ready?' Suddenly, the nose of the plane dipped. The fields came rapidly nearer, growing larger every second. The dive! Then the zoom climb. Now I saw nothing but sky and white cloud. A little later, the horizon appeared vertically. The vertical roll! I no longer had any sense of orientation, but I did not feel ill. The plane was full of tricks. Suddenly, I saw Mount Tsukuba in front of me. It was a much smaller mountain than Mount Fuji, but with a curiously similar silhouette. I tried to remember how mysterious Mount Fuji had looked, but the instructor's voice interrupted: 'I am letting go of the stick. You will fly towards Mount Tsukuba.'

The mountain was ahead of us, a little to the right. I pushed the rudder bar in this direction, but overdid it. The plane pitched. And suddenly one wing lifted. Anxiously, I pulled the stick towards me. The nose jerked up sharply and then the earth vanished! I lost sight of Mount Tsukuba completely.

'Easy now!' shouted Furuya. 'The rudder of a plane is much more sensitive than a glider's. You must allow for that!'

After twenty minutes' flying, we began the descent. As we approached the ground, I could clearly see the grasses bending in the wind. It was as if the focus of a lens was being adjusted. Below 300 feet, one had to judge altitude partly by looking at the vegetation.

During the flight, I had been outside myself so to speak. To be frank, I had not been able to watch the instrument panel calmly.

Beneath the awning, the young pilots were talking in low voices, exchanging impressions of their first flight. Even Cadet Pilot Yamada, in spite of his playful temperament, looked serious and intent. 'You know,' murmured Kagawa, 'I can understand what Flying Officer Komorizono meant now, you really have to drive all other concerns out of your mind.' I agreed with him. The evening before, Komorizono had said to us: 'Your hearts must be as pure as the sky. When you're piloting a plane, the least impurity will fester and lead you to your death. Forget your family, your girl friend, your studies . . . everything to do with your civilian life . . . in order to dedicate yourselves to flying. Nothing is more futile than to get yourself killed during a training flight.'

From the next day on, we had to fly in circles over the airfield. One tour took seven minutes: five tours per day. The propeller produces a torque effect, and on take-off it is always necessary to adjust the direction of the nose in terms of its effect on the directional rudder. At the beginning, we were troubled by this awkward effect that made taking-off more difficult than landing, but we gradually grew accustomed to making the necessary compensations.

Below the fourth turning-point of our circles, we could see a capricious little stream winding along, and some boys bathing in the water without a care in the world. This scene evoked dreams of one's own childhood. One day, as I started to volplane down with the throttle reduced, I began thinking of my own sister, who must be about the same age. From very close up, I suddenly saw human figures scattering in all directions. They were *shonen-hikoheis* who were training on gliders in a corner of the airfield. My glide path was too steep. 'What are you trying to do, kill them?' yelled the instructor behind me. But it would have been dangerous to jerk the stick back, as it might have entailed a fatal loss of speed. At full throttle, I elevated the nose of the plane gently, to start my landing approach again. At that moment, it really sank into my consciousness that a pilot is constantly threatened by death. Komorizono was quite right to say to us all the time: 'When you are flying, a moment's thoughtlessness can be fatal. Think of nothing but your manoeuvres, let nothing distract you, nothing! Death is lying in wait for you all the time. And always keep your belongings in order, so that they will not shame you if your fellow-pilots have the task of sending them to your families.'

I made a vow never again to let my mind wander during a flight.

It was on July 13 that we were informed of the defeat of Saipan. Our General Staff had already made the alarming decision, on June 24, that the island should be abandoned before mid-July. Knowing nothing of this terrible decision, and still hoping to receive arms and food supplies, our soldiers in Saipan dug in. The enemy was incontestably superior in men and materials. On July 6, both General Saito and Admiral Nagumo committed suicide.

The most frightful scenes followed: soldiers blew themselves up with grenades. Even civilians rushed headlong to their deaths; some women, cut off at Marpi point, took their children in their arms and leapt from the cliff tops, a height of some 500 feet. Others, arm in arm, waded out to sea and drowned, rather than submit to utter humiliation. What an appalling sight: imagine a mother throwing herself into the sea with her child in her arms! The Americans, furious with the Japanese on the island and relentless in their policy of genocide, should have been moved by the terrifying and yet dignified spectacle of death . . . [Because few Japanese would surrender the Americans had no option but to kill them. Editor.]

On July 9, Admiral Spruance, commander-in-chief of the Saipan operation, announced the conquest of the island. Out of 32,000 Japanese, there were only a thousand or so survivors. Because of the fear of public reaction, the General Staff did not announce the loss of Saipan until nine days later. And indeed it was this that forced Prime Minister Tojo to hand in his resignation on July 18.

We were staggered at this dreadful news. It was the decisive turning point in the Battle of the Pacific. After Saipan, our navy had only four aircraft carriers left, and there were not more than 2,500 aircraft in all. It was obvious that Japan had no hope at all of regaining supremacy on the sea or in the air. In the winking of an eye, the Americans would build a base for their B-29s, and Superfortress raids on Tokyo were now a foregone conclusion. The American fighters, based on aircraft carriers, would also very soon put in an appearance over the mainland. How could our little fighters measure up to this giant, the B-29, which could fly at a great altitude?

'Oh,' said Kagawa, 'our *Hayabusa* fighter, the "Falcon", could very well fight a B-29. The enemy can't have unlimited numbers of them. A *Hayabusa* against a B-29! In the end, they would destroy each other.'

His eyes shone. Was he already thinking of sacrificing his life for his country? If anyone but Kagawa had put forward such a suggestion, it would have seemed like succumbing to despair.

'But it's not easy to train pilots,' I answered him. 'We are indispensable to our country's defence. We must not throw our lives away lightly. The enemy will go on building more and more of these bombers, for they have almost infinite material resources. And that's all the more reason for staying alive and carrying on the struggle.'

'How else can we bring down these fabulous machines? Do you think our ack-ack [anti-aircraft fire] is efficient? These monsters fly at thirty thousand feet! Isn't it better to die than to let our dear country be devastated by enemy bombers?'

It was an unanswerable question. In actuality, a small fighter was not capable of reaching a high altitude and staying there long enough to engage in a dog fight. Perhaps the only way to destroy the B-29 was indeed to hurl oneself against it.

We were at an impasse. The partisans of an immediate and unconditional surrender might soon persuade the stubborn *zol*. [*zol* – from the German *Soldat* was used to describe the fanatical military caste.] This odious idea crossed my mind for an instant. A few nights earlier, I had had a dream: I saw myself standing in the classroom of the university, dressed in a student's uniform. As Freud says, the dream is a wish-fulfillment. So, I was still longing to go back to my studies. I was unconsciously hoping to be demobilised, while in my conscious mind I was determined to offer up my life in the service of my country. This moral dilemma could have a baleful effect on my concentration while flying.

To drive away my fear, I had only to remember that the U.S. bombers were threatening the cities on the Japanese archipelago.

Not one of us had so far been allowed to fly solo. We still had six months' training to undergo at the flying school. Would we be ready in time to confront the Superfortresses? Wouldn't it be too late? I was burning with impatience.

It was early August. The rainy season was over. On these fine summer days, a sultry sun blazed down on the runway. Just as we were about to take off, Komorizono said to us: 'Cadet Pilots Kagawa, Ono, Nagatsuka, Goto . . . you are to fly solo from now on. Whatever you do, don't lose your nerve! All you have to do is fly exactly as if the instructor were sitting at the dual controls.'

44

At last, the long-awaited solo flight! I had nine hours' flying to my credit. Watanabe and Takebuchi had flown solo the day before.

I settled myself, rather excitedly, into the pilot's seat. A sandbag had been placed on the instructor's seat to balance the aircraft. I warmed up the motor, checked temperature and oil pressure, tested the movements of the control column. As a final check, I revved up the engine, then . . . full throttle and away! Gaining momentum, I gently elevated the nose of the plane as it reached lift-off speed. Climbing now . . . altitude 750 feet! At the first turning point, I saw that the ball in the turn-and-slip indicator was moving towards the inner arc of the turn instead of remaining in the centre. The wind, striking from the side, was causing the plane to drift. I coolly adjusted the controls to compensate for this. The ball came back to the middle, and from then on it was a smooth and level flight!

I could see over a vast area, with mountains here and there on the horizon. Diaphanous clouds wafted swiftly across the sky. The artificial horizon was in its correct place. I felt fresh and alert and inwardly calm. It was a calm I had never experienced when at the dual controls. I looked below me. A railway line stretched across the fields, straight and level, and a string of carriages was rolling along. I caught sight of some white shirts as passengers leaned out of the windows and waved. Not daring to waggle my wings in response, I looked enviously at them. I remembered something Watanabe had said the day before: 'You know, when I see white shirts, I am seized with longing to wear civilian clothes. Isn't that a tiresome thing for an airman?' It was, to say the least, out of place in the atmosphere in which we lived. It was our duty to put all thoughts of civilian life out of our minds, once and for all.

Then came the landing. The plane was placed in the glide path. My angle of descent was correct. I approached the tarmac at the lowest possible speed . . . thirty feet . . . fifteen feet . . . The touch-down should be made at three points: both wheels of the undercarriage and the tail wheel. I pulled the stick slightly towards my stomach. Bump! And the plane rolled smoothly along the ground.

Happy and proud of having made a three-point landing, I reported to Komorizono: 'Cadet Pilot Nagatsuka. Overhead circling flight completed. All in order!'

'No!' he thundered. 'The tip of your wing was over the

dividing line between the take-off area and the landing area! If there had been a plane taking off just then, you would have collided. A disastrous fault!'

I had been totally unaware of this. No doubt he was right. A second later, I found myself on the floor – his fist had struck me full in the face. My head was spinning and my cheek on fire. He had hit hard. Nevertheless, I leapt up nimbly and at once. Komorizono was looking through binoculars, keeping an eye on the other planes in the sky. 'Do you understand?' he said, keeping the binoculars glued to his eyes. 'Good! You may dismiss.'

Returning to the hut where we awaited our turn to fly, I thought it over. Perhaps I had been so preoccupied with the touch-down that I had failed to notice the line of demarcation. I had no reason to suppose he was mistaken. On account of this error, my joy of being allowed to fly solo instantly evaporated. But I felt no rancour towards him. On the contrary, I told myself repeatedly; 'Avoid making that mistake in the future!'

That was the first and last time I was struck in the face at the training school. Theoretically, except in a very few cases, corporal punishment was strictly prohibited in flying schools as it would not do to try the nerves of pilots unduly.

It amazes me that still, in the present day, and even amongst our intellectual compatriots, there are those who make wounding and unjust remarks about the suicide-pilots who died so nobly. They were stupid, it is said, allowing themselves to be sacrificial victims to the ambitions of the military caste, in spite of the merciless treatment they received in the army. I make no secret of the fact that I detest the hypocrisy of these pacifists, who think it necessary to put military life on trial although they understand nothing of what went on in the hearts and minds of pilots at that time. The journalist Toshiro Takagui, writes in his work *Chiran*:

'The absolute necessity for training pilots quickly led to the most inhuman and outrageous abuses. This inhumanity, and the courage to carry it out, passed under the name of "patriotism". Flying Officer Jiro Ono, in charge of training the *tokusos* of the second intake, invariably carried a heavy bamboo cane in his hand, and used it with the utmost cruelty. As a graduate of the army flying school, it may be that he was a fanatical instructor. Whatever the reason, he was a ferocious

46

beast. Hardly any of the *tokusos* belonging to the *Chiran* corps escaped the blows of that cane.

'One evening, he punished eight cadets for indiscipline. With unimaginable violence, each man was punched in the face three hundred times: their teeth were broken, their mouths streamed blood, and their faces were so swollen they could no longer open their eyes. Next day, they were still prostrate, unable to put one foot in front of the other.

'In spite of this atrocity, they completed their training at Chiran and went on to perfect their flying technique in other aviation corps.'*

What a vile distortion of the truth! The author can have no idea how much pain these lying assertions give to the families of suicide-pilots killed on special missions. What a shock it would be to them if they sincerely believed their husband or son had been submitted to such brutal treatment before becoming a divine protector of his country!

'In his diary,' pursues the same author, 'Leading Aircraftman Kimura notes: "The instructors punish the *shonen-hikohei* incessantly, even during the actual flights. The pilot's seat in the trainers is always stained with blood. They are beaten with sticks, from behind, and threatened: 'For God's sake! Jump, you fool!' " In Kimura's squad, several had indeed jumped out of the plane and killed themselves. Suicides and desertions multiplied.

'Kimura was not the only one to undergo this appalling experience, it was general amongst trainee pilots and in the Japanese Army.'

Such a twisting of the facts is inadmissible. I can say nothing of the infantry, having had no experience in it, but to my knowledge this barbarous and idiotic cruelty never existed in the air force. Komorizono sometimes punched a young pilot, but never more than once. The other officers, from the commanding officer down, never brutalised them at all.

On that evening, when training was over and I was changing out of my summer suit and into uniform, a soldier came into the billets and said to me: 'Flying Officer Komorizono wants to see you, cadet pilot!'

Was he going to haul me over the coals again? I hurried

*Chiran, published by Asahi Shimbun Sha, 1965, pp. 22–23, Chiran is a small town in Southern Fyushu, from April 1945, many suicide-pilots took off on their final mission from the air base there.

nervously to his office, saying in my innermost self: 'I realise I was in the wrong. Is it necessary to punish me again?' I stood at attention before him. With a smile on his lips, he said: 'I hurt you, didn't I?'

'Yes, sir,' I replied, beaming. 'It was the first time I'd been hit since I enlisted.'

No resentment against him. The blow had been a punishment for my fault, that was all there was to it.

'Let's hope it will be the last,' he said, bursting out laughing. 'An officer must deliberately cultivate hardness of heart, he must avoid pity. Apart from that one mistake, your landing was impeccable! Don't forget to handle the rudder carefully. Here is your reward.'

He held out a huge bag of biscuits. How good of him! Extremely stern during training, a loyal officer whose reactions were simple and direct, he was at bottom a tender-hearted man. He always took an interest in his subordinates, even to the extent of occasionally evading the excessively harsh orders of Squadron Leader Watanabe. It was also thanks to his insistence that cadets were allowed one day's rest per month. On the odd occasions when he replaced a regular instructor, he always spoke very softly, but on the ground he roared like a bull! He knew exactly how to handle his men and bring out all their natural abilities as pilots.

Nevertheless, the training and our daily life were arduous. From 4.30 a.m., or from 6 a.m. at the latest, till curfew at 9 p.m., the young pilots had not a moment to themselves. Every minute of free time had to be devoted to polishing flying boots, cleaning goggles, burnishing swords, washing clothes and so on. Anyone who did have a free moment made use of it to get in some simulated flying practice, utilising the mock-up pilot's seats placed along the corridor. We all wanted passionately to make good progress. We enjoyed the privileges of a specially nourishing diet and a bottle of whisky every week, but in spite of this, our life was too demanding and tended to make the men morose. As Lafcadio Hearn, the English novelist who became a naturalised Japanese, said in his essay 'A Japanese Smile', our compatriots love to smile, if only to hide their suffering. But we had forgotten how to smile, there was no time. There were rumours that several cadet pilots attached to the navy had deserted, and it may be thought strange that there

48

were no desertions amongst our *tokusos*, who bore their sufferings bravely.

One morning, a plane approached the landing strip in a faulty position. 'Bring up the nose! Gently!' shouted Komorizono into the microphone. It was Ishikawa's plane. Boom! It stood on its nose and then flopped over on its back! Since it was a biplane, the pilot's life was not in danger. We glanced furtively at Squadron Leader Watanabe, who was purple in the face with rage and indignation. He shouted at the top of his voice: 'Ten thousand yens wasted!' and Ishikawa visibly shrivelled before him.

Thereupon, Komorizono shouted an order: 'Line up! Ten times round the airfield, at the double!' Swiftly saluting the squadron leader, he led the column of trainees off at a run. A timely manoeuvre! Komorizono really possessed the art of doing the appropriate thing at the opportune moment. If he had not thought of this dodge, who knows how far Watanabe's fury would have carried him?

Fifth time round . . . sixth time . . . the sun was burning hot. In our summer suits we were melting like snowballs in the sun. We were out of breath. As we finished the tenth circle, Komorizono was the first to sit down on the parched grass. We formed a circle round him, gasping for breath. He looked us over before speaking.

'Cadet Pilot Ishikawa,' he said sharply, 'it's your fault. Be careful when you're at the controls, and never let your thinking get woolly, do you understand? People tend to get incautious after fifteen or twenty hours' flying. Keep on your toes and don't relax your concentration for a moment. From tomorrow, we shall be doing aerobatics, I don't want any accidents . . .'

His manner was sharp, penetrating and icy, reflecting the impersonal severity of the army. Then he softened a little:

'Now listen,' he added. 'I have one more thing to say to you: when you become pilots, never sleep with a woman who is menstruating. If you ignore this tradition, you will run the risk of a flying accident. Perhaps it's just a superstition, but there have been many cases that could only be accounted for by this bizarre explanation. Many of those involved in accidents had ignored this legend. Try not to fall into the same errors as your predecessors.'

He stressed these last words with great seriousness, but his eyes were laughing. And what a shout of laughter from us!

4

No doubt he wanted to break the tension by making a joke. We listened to him carelessly, not knowing that his prediction would come true later on.

Training in aerobatics commenced with a vertical roll. Then came looping the loop, inverted flight, the Immelmann (stall turn), the horizontal roll and the slow barrel. These aerobatic tricks really made us feel like seasoned pilots. With each change in the plane's position, nature took on a new aspect. In the spiral dive, she seemed menacing, in the wing-over, indifferent. When I was flying, I had the sensation of being suspended between heaven and earth and of being propelled through a region which could contain only mystery or the void.

During my first aerobatic flights, I told myself that, in all this silent immensity, I had nothing to count on but my machine. Little by little, I began to conceive the idea that the 'I' had to blend with this mass of matter that was entirely at the mercy of nature. Moreover, the 'I' should not strive too hard to impose itself. Was it therefore impossible to succeed by the sheer force of one's own will? Yes, the only way was to put oneself entirely into nature's hands. Everything depended on her; in this sense, she had a more powerful influence over men than over trees!

In the evenings, we could hear the shrill chirping of the cicadas in the grove behind the billets. Wild and deafening music. They sang of the joy of living, ephemeral though it might be. Some would run out of breath but, inspired by the others, they soon began shrilling again with all their strength. Their song awoke profound reverberations within me; perhaps this was the last time I would hear them. . . . A pilot's life was no more enduring than that of the cicadas with their brief music.

At the end of August came the first day for family visits. I had sent my parents a note informing them of it. Was I really going to see them again? I could not believe it. At that time, it was extremely difficult to get hold of a railway ticket, since we had few trains, and 80 per cent of those few were commandeered for the transport of troops. With beating hearts, we awaited the soldier responsible for announcing visitors. At half past ten, he stood on the threshold of the sleeping quarters and intoned: 'Cadet Pilot Nagatsuka, your family has just arrived!' I rushed into the reception hall and found my mother and my three sisters. It was only three months since we had parted, and yet it seemed to me years and years. I suddenly found that my mother had aged. She was overwhelmed with cares: the family was about to leave Nagoya, because of the threat of air raids, and my mother was desperately looking for a house in the country.

She looked into my eyes. No words of mine can express the pathos of a mother who must resign herself to awaiting the death of her son; her eyes filled with a thousand emotions. It was a dazzling, sublime look. I gave her a military salute.

'Ah,' she murmured, 'you are a real officer.'

'You think so, mother? As for the army . . .'

I hesitated. I would have liked to talk to her about the contradictions in my own mind, the harshness of a pilot's life, the lamentable state of the war. But it would only add to her sorrow and anxiety and give her morbid ideas. She did not seem to understand and changed the subject:

'You know, I've just found a temporary place for us in the country. We shall be moving as soon as we get home. Here is our new address.'

'But . . . what about our house in Nagoya?' I asked.

'Oh, no doubt it will go to rack and ruin, since we'd never be able to find a tenant at a time like this. Or it will be destroyed by bombs. Recently, we've had civilian air raid drills almost every day. Even the children have been given instructions. Every family has to build an air raid shelter in the garden. Because of the manpower shortage, your sisters and I had to dig out ours . . .'

Eiko interrupted my mother:

'Oh, listen!' she shouted. 'Can't we go inside an airplane?'

'Right!' I said. 'Let's go and sit by the planes.'

The reception hall was already full of people. I led my family towards a transport plane. N.C.O.'s and soldiers who passed us saluted me. I felt embarrassed returning their salute. My mother stopped each time and bowed low. She was no doubt astonished to see N.C.O.'s who were so much older than I pay such respect to her son.

We sat down under the wing of a two-engined transport plane, a Ki-54. All our aircraft were designated by the secret appellation Ki, followed by a number. For example, the *Hayabusa* (Falcon) was called Ki-43, the *Akatonbo* (Dragonfly) was the Ki-9.

51

My mother opened a large bag and took out four bottles of beer, some *manjus* and iced cakes. I opened my eyes wide in surprise.

'Look,' said my eldest sister, 'Mother has worked miracles for you. The food situation is getting worse and worse. You can't find cigarettes any more. She is convinced you don't get enough to eat and she worries about you.'

I turned and looked at my mother in gratitude. My heart was so full that I could not contain it any longer – I stood up abruptly and ran towards the barracks. In my room, I gathered up what was left of my rations: chocolates, a bottle of whisky, some tins of nourishing foodstuffs. I had put them aside for my family.

Before giving them to my mother, I said: 'Now don't worry, Mother! Pilots are very well fed, and here's the proof. Take all this for my sisters and keep the things you brought me. You are the ones who are in need.'

While we were picnicking in the open air, someone spoke from behind me. It was Kagawa.

'Allow me to sit with you (*kisama*),' he said. 'I didn't ask my people to come because I was afraid it would be too upsetting. But I'm feeling a bit blue. . . . ' I invited him to share our meal, then introduced him to my mother and sisters.

'I don't like that officer,' Eiko whispered. 'He addresses my brother by the familiar form, it is not nice.'

Kagawa heard her. 'Excuse me, Miss, but it is the custom amongst Japanese soldiers,' he said. Then he took some chocolates and cakes out of his pocket. 'Here, take these!' he said. Eiko's red face made us laugh. Yes, we actually laughed a good, loud laugh! I exchanged an astonished look with Kagawa. How long was it now since we had laughed? Eiko's open, childish face had suddenly brightened our grim existence as soldiers. It was like a refreshing shower after drought.

When we had eaten, I showed my two little sisters the interior of the Ki-54. They were full of wonder, never having seen a plane close to before. The time passed quickly. At three o'clock, I accompanied my family as far as the gate. We walked slowly. My mother stopped for a moment to tell me in a voice heavy with tears: 'Your cousin Hideo was killed in battle in Saipan. The authorities notified your aunt ten days ago. It is sad news.

I did not know how to answer her. We were following the

52

path that led from the airfield to the entrance to the barracks. We had not been speaking, for our hearts, bursting with a thousand emotions, preferred to keep silence. We left each other with great regret in front of the sentry. I watched my family moving away into the distance. Oh, the sorrow of those farewells! At the moment when all four bowed to me before vanishing at the end of the road, I could no longer hold back my tears.

After lights-out, I could not get to sleep. The image of my family was constantly before my eyes: my mother, looking at me with such affection in her eyes, my sisters examining the interior of the Ki-54 with such innocent happiness. Would this ghastly war finally deprive them too of the hope of a carefree life? My cousin Hideo, a lieutenant in the Imperial Army, killed in Saipan. And next it would be my turn! I imagined my parents, with tears streaming down their faces, as they read the fatal communiqué reporting my death on active service. The upbringing of their only son had given them a reason for living. I could not help thinking what a void my death would leave in their lives.

We had applied ourselves relentlessly to our training, and now just a few hours of nostalgia in the company of our families threatened to undermine our discipline and our identity as officers! I sought to justify my human sentiments in my own mind.

Wing Commander Kato, director of the flying school of Utsunomiya, would have liked us all to discard our individual personalities and our sentiments. He had recently declared: 'Human personality counts for nothing! Flying skill is all that matters. We need good pilots rather than good officers. The vital thing is for the air force to turn out pilots who can shoot down the maximum number of enemy planes. What does it matter if they are not outstanding individuals from a humanist point of view?' Perhaps he was exaggerating a little. On the other hand, the army and its frightful slaughter might well be considered alien to humanity.

About ten days later, I was standing under the awning waiting for my turn to fly. By this time, we had all been allowed to go solo for aerobatic flights. Suddenly, I saw a brown mass thrown into the air near the awning. Then it fell and lay still on the ground. Yamada, who had been standing on the waiting line, had had the misfortune to be struck by the propeller of a taxiing plane. Everyone rushed over to him. He had been killed instantaneously. His neck had been split open like a pomegranate. I stared wide-eyed at the horrible, preposterous sight: blood vessels around the cervical vertebrae were spouting blood as if it were being pumped out by pumps of varying sizes. It was a revelation of the activity of innumerable cells, each one seeming to strive desperately to stay alive, although the body no longer showed signs of life. His goggles had been crushed to a powder. The first accident . . .

Komorizono ordered the ground crews, nicknamed 'beetles' in the aviation corps, to take the body to the infirmary. Assuming that flight training would be suspended, the cadet pilots lined up. Pale with rage, Komorizono fulminated: 'Who gave the order to suspend training? Get going immediately!' I was haunted by the words Yamada had whispered in my ear only moments before: 'When my turn comes, I'll do my favourite trick. Watch me carefully at five thousand feet.' Surely we had the right to pray for the repose of his soul, at least for a minute! The inhumanity of the army made me want to vomit. After Yamada, it was my turn to fly. Just as I was going to the plane, Komorizono called me over and said: 'Death is not uncommon in aviation. You must not pay it the least attention, otherwise there is a danger that you in your turn will cause another accident!'

That evening, we were filling in our flight cards in the study room. Our hearts were heavy. We were all thinking of the sudden death of Yamada. Flying Officer Haiji, leader of the 1st Squad, came in and said: 'The idea of death must not provoke in you that agitation that is natural to the human heart. I understand your feelings. But we are soldiers and must keep our will to conquer undiminished. We must be absolutely ready to act in the face of a thousand difficulties. It will not help to brood over Yamada's death. Instead, you must keep only one thought in your heads: to take his place and accomplish the task he can no longer fulfil.'

Two mornings later, I was on guard in full-dress uniform with another cadet pilot. Yamada had already been cremated and his ashes rested in a little wooden box covered with a white cloth. As there was no dry ice available, his body had been burned twenty-four hours after his death, without awaiting the arrival of his parents. I saw two people enter one of the hangars, where the altar stood in one corner. Yamada's parents. They had just come from Kyoto. Turned to stone in front of the altar, they gazed at it with that blank look that makes you think of the lustreless eyes of an ox standing motionless in a field. They were utterly expressionless, neither anger nor sorrow showed on their faces. It seems that an overwhelming affliction produces in man all the appearances of insensibility.

After the funeral rites had been carried out in the hangar, Yamada, or rather his remains, were to leave the flying school forever. His father held the box containing the ashes in his arms and carried it away to the strains of Chopin's 'Funeral March'. On the oblong label stuck to the box was written: 'The Late Flying Officer Michinori Yamada.' His promotion made us realise the vanity of military honours. We would never speak of him again.

At the begining of October, the days began to draw in. It is in autumn that man, beneath a cooling sun, reaps what he has sown. For us, the harvest marked one step nearer to death. One day, we cleaned our summer suits with especial care, the *tokusos* of the fourth and fifth intakes would have to wear them next spring, when they succeeded us. Then we went to the clothing depot to receive a winter flying suit, boots and fur-lined helmet. 'Look at us, dressed up like Eskimos!' somebody joked. This outfit made us heavy and clumsy, and I was even worried that it might hamper my movements in the cockpit.

A few days later, we began training in formation flying. We flew in formations of six. Flying Officer Haiji led my group. The distance between the wing tip of one plane and the next must always equal the span of the plane. 'In flight, follow me at all costs! Don't spread out!' That was Haiji's eternal refrain, and we obeyed it at the risk of crowding him too closely, almost touching. The leader joked about it: 'You'd think I was a pretty girl, with all her sweethearts hanging on to her skirt!' Normally, he would signal us when it was time to start the group aerobatic exercises, but sometimes he did it suddenly and without warning. Allez-oop! The 'rocket' climb! Some of the planes were slow to respond and the leading aircraft would be way up in front, much higher. Then the formation echelonned and fanned out correctly, our leader facilitating the regrouping movement by accelerating. Squadron Leader

Watanabe kept repeating: 'During a group attack, the leader of the formation will not have time to signal a change of direction. You must be ready at all times to react to his sudden manoeuvres!' He was right. During formation flying, it was essential to keep your eyes on your leader's plane as well as on the instrument panel. And therein lay the difficulty.

One morning, we were flying in this manner over Nikko, a very picturesque spot. It was that hour when dawn is chasing away the dusk and certain hues stand out brilliantly. Two years ago, at the same time of year, I had visited this region and been dazzled by the beauty of the russet leaves of autumn. Today, I glanced down at the mountains of Nikko. The same beautiful panorama unfolded before my eyes, but this time, I felt that I was looking at a mantle of blood. Of course, the foliage displayed the same bright and pleasing autumnal tones, but this time it reminded me of Yamada's body drenched in blood. The same colour in the landscape will evoke different images in a man's mind, depending on the state of his spirit. One might almost say that a landscape is the reflection of the moment.

The days seemed to drag on interminably, so impatient were we to fly faster planes – the Ki-55, Type 99.

One day, Flight Lieutenant Fukuchima's car stopped in front of the awning. He was the leader of the 2nd Squad, and had just had a secret interview with Squadron Leader Watanabe and Flying Officer Komorizono. All three looked tense and their abnormal pallor spoke of some unusual event. What had happened? 'Training suspended! Return to quarters!' said Komorizono simply and sullenly. An instructor grabbed the microphone and ordered all planes to land without delay. All engines stopped. This unusual silence was most ominous.

Half an hour later, all cadet pilots assembled in the study room. Squadron Leader Watanabe looked all round the room before starting to speak:

'Our fuel supplies are almost exhausted. For the moment, this flying school will not be receiving any more petrol. We are unfortunately compelled to suspend flying training until further orders. . . .'

It was a shock. We still had to learn navigation, flying in poor visibility and shooting in flight at the 'air sleeve' towed by a plane. What would we do without fuel? Would we be compulsorily grounded, instead of becoming combat pilots? At the moment, we were in the same wretched boat as the ground crews. Up to this time, those few cadet pilots who had been transferred to training schools for mechanics had been sent only because they lacked the qualities necessary to a pilot. How we looked down our noses at them!

Without our flying sessions, we felt lost and discouraged. Whole days were filled with lectures on navigation and night flying, and we were made to do bayonet practice. None of this excited our enthusiasm. This last exercise in particular depressed us, for it was infantry training. 'Hey,' said some of the men in despair, 'it looks as if we'll end up as foot-sloggers! We'll feel like fish out of water.'

Happily, flight training began again after a ten-day interval. But only one day out of five for each squad, and we no longer used normal aircraft fuel, but petrol mixed with alcohol – the so-called *A-Go* fuel. It had a much lower flash point than petrol and had to be handled with the utmost caution.

It was mid-November. Trainees from the 1st Squad were in the courtyard, resting between two courses. The sky above the roof of the barracks shone blue and serene. Some planes were performing aerobatics. 'Oh, God!' someone cried. 'There's one coming down!' A plane that had just completed the Immelmann manoeuvre was falling in a tail spin. Once the motor stalled, it was impossible to start it again with that confounded fuel! 'Press the rudder bar! Push the stick forward! Quick!' we all screamed at the top of our voices, knowing full well that the pilot could not hear us. It was important to stop the rotating movement by adjusting the directional controls and then reduce the angle of incidence little by little by pushing the stick forward. The plane was falling faster and faster. It had already started spinning like a top. It was too late! . . . 3,000 feet . . . 1,500 feet . . . 300 feet . . . It disappeared, leaving a trail in the sky. This was the second accident; the victim was Cadet Pilot Nakajima of the 3rd Squad.

In the days that followed, there were other accidents, resulting in three more deaths. Two trainees had to jump by parachute. The poor-quality fuel was the cause of all the difficulties. Gradually, we were hardening ourselves to the idea of death. By a process of conscientious self-deception, we tried to chase away the obsessive awareness that we lived under a perpetual threat. During flying sessions, we were alert and bright-eyed, but on the ground we were sick at heart.

Scarcely ten days had passed since we had witnessed Nakajima's fatal accident. I was flying my trainer at an altitude of 4,875 feet. Visibility was excellent. I checked the instrument panel to make sure everything was in working order before I began the aerobatic exercises. Everything was going fine. Barrel roll! The horizon swung over. I watched it fixedly: it was essential to keep one's sense of orientation. The plane was just reverting to a horizontal position. The angle was correct. I brought the aircraft up dead level. One must not pass zero degrees. At that moment, I saw a plane in front of me. Giving the engine full throttle, I began to chase it, considering it an enemy. I did not know whether it was Watanabe's plane or Kagawa's. Suddenly, it started to dive. Reducing engine speed, I followed. A few seconds later, my engine spluttered. I glanced at the luminous dial of the fuel gauge. Normal! It could not be a 'dry stall'. I instantly abandoned the idea of chasing my hypothetical adversary, who was rocketing up again. I pressed the throttle lever forward to lift the plane gradually. No, the engine went on spluttering! The revolution counts were rapidly decreasing. Altitude? . . . 2,500 feet!

There was nothing for it but to attempt a forced landing. Our aerodrome was in the opposite direction. The slightest adjustment of the steering controls would entail a fatal loss of speed, so it was out of the question to try landing on the runway. But I kept a cool head, and refused to parachute out: I just could not bring myself to let the plane crash. The engine was panting. I gently lowered the nose of the craft. Even in normal flight, the limits within which one can vary the angle of flight are critical. It was not easy to maintain a slight downward slope of the plane together with a low speed in a descending trajectory. I concentrated all my attention on the altitude and directional controls . . . 1,800 feet . . . 1,500 feet. I gave the motor full throttle again, but still it throbbed erratically. At an altitude of 750 feet, it cut out altogether. That damned A-Go fuel again! Nothing to be done but glide. As long as there were no obstacles at the end of my run! A fraction of a second's distraction and it would be disaster. I had already cut the magnetos. The harvested and harrowed fields stretched away beneath me. 30 feet . . . 15 feet. Now! I pulled the altitudinal controls towards my stomach. A juddering shock! The undercarriage stuck in the ruts of the harrow, and the plane did a nose stand. I felt a scorching pain in my right ankle, as if I had sprained it. I hastily undid my belt and jumped to the ground. Sitting down on the parched earth, I took off my boot and massaged my painful right ankle. Some rather aged peasants, who lived nearby, came running towards me. They looked at me inquisitively, perhaps expecting to find me gravely wounded. I sighed with relief, not in the least upset. One of the peasants offered to massage my leg.

Presently, a vehicle from the school arrived, equipped with an electric starting device. It was full of mechanics. 'You're not hurt, Cadet Pilot?' asked an N.C.O. 'No, I'm all right,' I said, standing up. But the shooting pains in my ankle made me limp. Leaning on his shoulder, I climbed into the truck.

Back at the training field, I reported the accident to Komorizono. 'Nothing serious?' he asked me. 'No, sir!' I said, but as I walked towards the bench under the awning, he stopped me. 'You're limping! What's the matter? Report to the infirmary immediately!' And in spite of my protestations, he insisted.

'It's only a sprain. Three days in the infirmary,' said the army doctor, after a rather brutal examination. In fact, all he did was twist my ankle while putting on a poultice. Far from being soothed, the pain seemed to intensify. A bruise was spreading up my leg. What a quack! I went into the rest room dragging my leg.

Next morning, Kagawa was kind enough to visit me. 'Better?' he asked. I thought he looked very down in the mouth.

'It's all right,' I said, 'not quite so painful. But what's wrong with you? Your face is as long as a fiddle.'

'Listen to this,' he said. 'Last night, Squadron Leader Watanabe gave us some bad news . . . the army can't possibly let us have any more fuel. We are to leave this school early in December and go on to advanced training in one of the front-line air corps. The squads are being reorganised. You are in the Third Squad, which will be sent to Kyushu.'

'Impossible! We haven't even finished our navigation course. And what about you?'

'I'm in the Second Squad. We're going to Korea.'

Originally, we were not due to leave the school until the end of January – now it had been put forward by two months! Nevertheless, we still had a lot of training to get through: study of armaments used on board aircraft, firing at the 'air sleeve', firing at a floating target and so forth. Were they going to assign us to fighting squadrons before we had completed this training? Only a few days to go and December would be upon us . . . no time to lose!

I changed quickly, with Kagawa's help, and presented myself in the sawbones' surgery. 'The pain has gone, sir! Would you please give me permission to leave the infirmary?' I asked him. He was reluctant, but I rushed out, in spite of the pain in my ankle, and went back to my billet. The list of the four newly formed squads had just been stuck up on a wall in the corridor. The 1st Squad was to be drafted to Formosa, the 2nd to Korea, the 3rd to Kyushu and the 4th to Kansai (the area which includes Osaka, Kyoto, Kobe, Nara, etc.). The names of the bases were not given. Departure date for the 3rd Squad was December 1. Kagawa's group was to leave for Korea on the 4th. And Watanabe? He was in the 1st Squad, due to leave Mibu on December 7. My heart turned over. I forgot the pain in my ankle.

Two days later, we took our first navigational test. The day before, we had attended the final lecture on theory. We had to fly as far as the aerodrome at Kanamaruhara. Luckily, the weather was clear that day. The planes took off at ten-minute intervals. My right ankle was not so painful, but I worried about it because the joint was ankylosed and felt as if it did not belong to me. 'Will I be able to take off with this blasted leg?' I wondered as I clambered into the cockpit. Engine purring, full throttle, control column towards the instrument panel. I pulled the craft up off the ground. I sighed with relief; the proverb was true: 'Fear magnifies everything.' The plane gained altitude steadily.

To the right, I could see Mount Tsukuba already covered in snow. I had become familiar with this mountain over the last five months, but perhaps I was seeing it now for the last time. I waggled my wings lightly by way of farewell, as if it had been a friend I was leaving. As my uncle's family lived in this region, I would have liked to fly down a little and wave goodbye.

This flight from one airfield to another did not present any problems, and I carried out my exercise quite successfully. Two questions still troubled me, however: Could I be certain of accurate navigation over the sea, since obviously a single exercise was not enough to accustom one to this task. Secondly, would my right leg impede my manoeuvres during flight, as it seemed to be paralysed and normal circulation had not been restored.

On the evening of November 30, I was busy preparing for our departure next day. Between roll call and curfew, Kagawa and Watanabe came into the quarters. They hurried up to me, and we looked at one another with full hearts. Our friendship had been a source of joy to me in this grey and bleak existence, where the absence of all human feeling was necessarily imposed on us. 'Till we meet again,' said our lips, but our eyes said 'Farewell.' Kagawa fumbled in a pocket of his flying suit and pulled out his fountain pen. Then he held it out to me and said solemnly: 'I have used this pen for a long time. I give it to you as a token of affection. Take it as a keepsake. Good luck! And may we all acquit ourselves bravely!'

One more minute and we would have been overcome with emotion. They left without another word. And so, in this rather hasty and furtive way, we parted.

The last night at Mibu passed, wiping out all passion, suffering, weariness and memory.

Part Two

All around me the sky was serene,
as if nothing had happened. . . .

Black, threatening clouds were gathering over Japan. On November 24, the capital had been the first target in an air raid carried out by ninety-four B-29 bombers from the Saipan base. The industrial district had taken the brunt of it. I hated to think that the enemy pilots had at last, and with the greatest of ease, seen our sacred Mount Fuji, and – oh, irony of Fate! – it had even served them as a landmark.

At the end of August, Prime Minister Kuniaki Koiso had made a shock announcement, warning the nation to stand firm and be ready for the approaching struggle, which would be decisive. Since the fall of Saipan, the newspapers had frequently declared that our positions had been deliberately established with a view to this decisive battle. They were trying to fortify the people and raise their morale. The next confrontation, it was hoped, would be a resounding success like Pearl Harbor. In spite of these exhortations, the climate was far from optimistic.

The attack on Formosa had begun on October 12. Three days later, Halsey's armada was attacked by nearly a hundred aircraft belonging to our 26th Naval Air Fleet, together with seventy army fighters, under the command of Rear Admiral Masabumi Arima. His advisers had tried to dissuade the Rear Admiral from taking part in this engagement personally, but in vain: he removed his insignia of rank and led the formation. Brave, intrepid and even reckless, he resolved to crash in flames on the deck of an enemy aircraft carrier. The same day, the Combined General Staff announced the remarkable results reported by our pilots: two aircraft carriers sunk and eight severely damaged. The entire population was jubilant. The Emperor addressed his sacred words to the Combined Fleet. Alas! The information was false. Our pilots were inexperienced and had not known how to verify the sinking of ships accurately; they had taken the waterspouts raised by our own crashing planes to be signs of enemy vessels going to the bottom. On October 20, the Americans landed on the beaches of Leyte, one of the Philippine Islands: ' . . . This is General MacArthur speaking to you. People of the Philippines, I have returned. By the grace of Almighty God, our forces have once again set foot on this soil consecrated by the blood of our two peoples. . . . ' Before sundown, the enemy had disembarked 60,000 men and occupied the airport of Tacloban.

Our mistaken assessment of the outcome of the Battle of Formosa led to a change of plan: whereas previously our military leaders had intended to mount a decisive battle in the island of Luzon, they now turned their eyes towards Leyte. Believing that the enemy naval force had been almost completely wiped out, they viewed the American assault on Leyte as a grave error – and prepared to take advantage of this folly. The Combined Fleet ordered Admiral Kurita to head for the Gulf of Leyte with the aim of destroying the enemy convoy. On October 22, the battleship *Musashi*, which was to act as a sort of decoy, was repainted light grey. The other ships were still dark grey and black. A petty officer on the *Musashi* remarked ironically: 'Here is a costume for dying in (*shini-shozoku*), since we have the fourth commander (*Shi*) and the second (*Ni*) second-in-command. What a coincidence!' In Japanese, *shini* means death and *shozoku* means costume. The crew laughed at the prediction, at once sinister and improbable, but two days later, alas! it came true.

During the night of the 22nd-23rd, Kurita's armada, sailing due north towards Mindoro, was spotted by two American submarines, the *Darter* and the *Dace*, which were in the straits of Palawan. When Admiral Halsey received this news, Admiral McCain's squadron, Task Force 38-1, was already making for Uliti harbour, where the crews were to rest, and was too far away to engage in the action. Determined to take personal command of the Task Force, Halsey posted Task Group 38-3 to the east of Luzon and Task Group 38-4 in the sea off Leyte. Task Group 38-2, under the command of Rear Admiral Bogan, was sent out to sea in the Strait of San Bernardino. This group was later to be the target for my suicide mission.

At 0520 on the 23rd, Kurita's squadron was attacked by the two American submarines. The heavy cruiser *Atago*, flying Vice Admiral Kurita's ensign, as well as the heavy cruiser *Maya* were sent to the bottom. The Admiral was picked up by the destroyer *Kishinami* and transferred to the battleship *Yamato* at 1523. These losses were to weigh heavily against us in the outcome of the battle.

Next morning, Kurita's forces advanced into the waters of Mindoro. Battleships *Yamato* and *Musashi,* surrounded by other vessels, were silhouetted majestically against the golden horizon. Each of these big ships had a tonnage of 69,100 tons and was armed with nine guns of 460 millimetres.

Without air cover, the *Musashi* played the part of a deliberate decoy, for which role she had specifically been repainted, and drew most of the enemy's fire. Thanks to her heavy guns, she was prepared for a battle to the death. At 0810, a reconnaissance plane from Bogan's force discovered our armada and sent the message: 'Detected to the south of Mindoro: four battleships, eight cruisers, thirteen destroyers. Heading fifty degrees. Speed ten to twelve knots.' Halsey telegraphed King, Kinkaid and Nimitz to tell them of the discovery of the Japanese flotilla. He ordered McCain's forces to do an about-turn and Task Groups 38-3 and 38-4 to rejoin Bogan. At 0845, three aircraft carriers of Task Group 38-2, the *Intrepid,* the *Cabot* and the *Independence,* launched the first assault, with thirty-one fighters, twelve dive bombers and eighteen torpedo bombers. It was at 0925 that these sixty-one planes arrived above the objective. The *Musashi* remained imperturbable. The second wave, consisting of thirty-five planes from Bogan's force, obtained better results. The *Musashi* was hit by three torpedoes and two bombs.

By the time a fourth attack had been carried out, the battleship was beginning to founder at the bows, although her anti-aircraft guns were still sending up a massive cone of fire. Rear Admiral Inokuchi, commanding the *Musashi,* committed hara-kiri at the moment when the waves engulfed his ship at 1837 in the Sea of Sibugan. Thus, our navy lost one of the two giant battleships of which she was so proud.

On the morning of the same day, 199 planes of our 2nd Naval Air Fleet, land-based in the Philippines, attacked Task Group 38-3, which was to the east of Luzon. The aircraft carrier *Princeton* was sunk, the light cruiser *Birmingham* and three destroyers were damaged. At 1245, the second wave of 76 planes attacked the same Task Group. These planes had left Ozawa's squadron and were making for the base at Luzon.

This attack, however, alerted the Americans to the presence of our aircraft carriers, commanded by Admiral Ozawa. Halsey was therefore aware of our three fleets converging on the scene of the battle: Kurita's coming from the west, Ozawa's from the north and Nishimura's from the south. He sent this information to Admiral Kinkaid, commander-in-chief of the 7th Fleet, who had under his orders the escorting aircraft carriers commanded by Admiral Sprague, which were to the east of the Gulf of Leyte, and the battleship flotilla commanded by Admiral Oldendorf, which was in Surigao Strait. In the course of the battle against Oldendorf's flotilla, which broke out at midnight, Admiral Nishimura lost all his ships with the exception of one destroyer which was forced to leave the battle area after suffering serious damage.

At 0644 on the 25th, Kurita's armada discovered an enemy force to the southeast of the island of Samar: six escorting aircraft carriers, three destroyers and four escort destroyers under the command of Rear Admiral Clifton Sprague.

Admiral Kurita worked out a prudent tactic: to destroy the flight decks of the enemy carriers first of all by fire from our battleships and cruisers. Then torpedoes launched from our destroyers would be able to finish them off.

At 0658, the *Yamato* opened fire with her huge guns, at a range of 40,000 yards. Our ships put on all speed to bear down on the foe, who was already beginning to flee. At about 0800 hours, our battleship *Kongo* attacked the aircraft carrier *Gambier Bay* and sent her to the bottom. Then the destroyer *Hoel*, hit by a heavy shell from the *Yamato*, was seen to founder. Two aircraft carriers, under punishment from the tremendous salvoes, were put out of action. Two other destroyers, the *Samuel B. Roberts* and the *Johnston*, were also sunk. Kinkaid had sent Halsey a message calling for immediate assistance. The latter took not the slightest notice, for his 34th Task Force was already fully engaged with Ozawa's armada. However, he left the battle area and rushed towards the San Bernardino Strait. But out at sea, beyond the Gulf of Leyte, the situation had been transformed: at 0911, Kurita's force withdrew. Sprague's group, whose annihilation had seemed inevitable, finally managed to take shelter in the Gulf of Leyte. The destroyers in Kurita's squadron were short of fuel. The Admiral judged it too dangerous to indulge in battle in the well-fortified gulf, where the manoeuvring of his ships would be strictly limited, so he steered north to locate the enemy task force. And thus, in effect, terminated the great naval battle of the Philippines. Balance-sheet: thirty of our ships lost, including three battleships, as against the loss of six American ships.

At 0530 on December 1, twenty-seven cadet pilots of the 3rd Squad left the flying school to take the train to Utsunomiya. How many times had I dreamed of travelling on this train that linked Utsunomiya to Koga, the little town where my uncle lived! But without leave, a visit to my uncle's family was just a utopian dream. And we were not taking the train to Koga, but in the opposite direction. A wall of earth separated us from the rest of the world and all those creatures who were dear to me were slipping farther and farther away.

In the compartment, we looked nostalgically at the civilians. The impulse to speak to them was almost irresistible, but of course it was strictly forbidden. Like the men, the women wore trousers, which allowed them greater freedom of movement, and the men wore khaki clothing and carried steel helmets. Everybody was on a war footing!

At Usunomiya station, we took another train which was to take us to Tokyo. It was cold and there was no heating in the carriage. The train cut across the countryside and I saw the same landscape that I had seen from a plane, though it looked quite different. The white mists of winter frayed and hovered like wisps of smoke. I gazed towards the spot where I had made a forced landing, but it was invisible behind veils of fog. Suddenly I thought of my right leg, which was still rather swollen. I was obsessed by the idea that it might be a hindrance to me when I was eventually engaged in an air battle. Unconsciously, I massaged my leg with my right hand. All my companions were preoccupied with their own thoughts.

At Tokyo, we changed again for Kyushu. As soon as we had settled into our seats, two policemen appeared and spoke to Flying Officer Imamura, who was escorting us to the base.

'Flying Officer,' they said, saluting and standing at attention, 'you are requested to pull down the blinds and keep them down until the train reaches its destination. The transfer of your cadets is a military secret and they should not be seen by civilians. It is strictly prohibited for them to enter other compartments, and they must not allow any civilian to enter theirs.

Every six hours, at the principal stations, the police will issue you rations.'

We were in fact wearing pilots' insignia on our chests to distinguish ourselves from other soldiers. We hastily drew down the blinds. We had plenty of room, whereas the civilians were crammed into other carriages or even standing for the whole journey. We felt sorry for them. Soon after departure, Flying Officer Imamura gathered us around him:

'And now,' he said, 'I can tell you which base you have been assigned to.'

His voice was calm. There was a moment of absolute silence, then a wave of murmurs. Were we to be sent to some base in the Philippines which was on the eve of a decisive battle? He revealed to us that we were going to the 4th Squadron base at Ozuki. 'Their planes are the Ki-45 Kais, twin-engined fighters. They're called *Toryu*, and are destined to fight the B-29.' *Toryu* means the slaying of a dragon. Imamura went on: 'The dragon we have to slay in the immediate future is, as I said, the Superfortress, the "Flying Dragon", and training will begin as soon as you reach the base. Now, get all the rest you can during the journey. And . . . best of luck!'

We had all greeted this news enthusiastically. On June 16, eight Ki-45 Kais based at Ozuki had carried off a remarkable victory, knocking out four B-29s and damaging three above Yahata. Moreover, the B-29s of 20th Bomber Command, flying from the Chengtu base in China, had been invading the skies over Kyushu incessantly. Out of the ninety-four Superfortresses that bombed Tokyo on November 24, only twenty-four had succeeded in reaching the airplane engine factories which were the objective. Dropping their bombs from a height of over 30,000 feet, their aim was obviously lacking in precision. And, formidable though they were, there must be a means of bringing them down. We were convinced of it.

We could not enjoy the landscape because of the lowered blinds. Having no newspapers or magazines, I closed my eyes and folded my arms, trying to doze. For the first time in six months, I knew what it was to relax. I thought about my part in the war, my predetermined role as a pilot. What was the good of self-righteously damning the machines of war that were spreading ruin and misery? I was part of it, and, as a fighting pilot, would be forced to look at death from close to. I dreamed of it constantly. Perhaps the civilian passengers were able to shed their cares as they gazed out of the windows and lose themselves in the contemplation of nature. I envied them.

For myself, the image of death was symbolised by a little black speck, glued to my retina, which floated before my eyes day and night like an indefatigable gnat. It did not buzz, it did not sting, but was all the more deadly for that. Just as I was about to catch it, it dodged nimbly away and hid itself somewhere, in the corner of my eye. A totally elusive foe. I could not think of anything without this little dot appearing in the void. Was it really floating before my eyes, or was it stuck on to my pupils? It seemed to be mocking me. Death was not present in my mind in any concrete form. I did not visualise the tragic scene in which I would die, nor picture my wretched corpse. But this abstract, hallucinatory vision certainly existed and I could not get rid of it! At times, the minute black speck grew larger and turned crimson, no doubt reminding me of the scarlet cells pulsating with life in Yamada's dead body. Enlarged and suddenly bleeding, it looked like a red balloon, flaccid and partly deflated. Its slow transition from a liquid to a solid state was macabre and threatening. Obscene and oppressive, it seemed to gulp down its most vulnerable victim in the twinkling of an eye. Terrorised, I would have convulsions during my nightmares, and then reality and the morbid vision became confused. I could not escape the sight of death at close quarters. All images are surely the expression of the state of one's soul.

I was shaking my head once more in the hope of driving away the sinister apparition when someone tapped my knee. It was Cadet Pilot Furukawa.

'Tell me,' he said earnestly, 'didn't Flight Sergeant Nonaka, who crashed his plane into a B-29 in October, belong to the Fourth Squadron? Well, then, that's the very best method of bringing down those damned planes. All we have to do is follow his example!'

I thought he must be hiding a certain despair under such enthusiasm. I flushed angrily, hesitated, then shrugged my shoulders. I looked at him coolly and saw that my look embarrassed him a little. Flight Sergeant Nonaka had rammed his Ki-45 Kai into the mammoth bomber to bring it down. He had been promoted two grades at once. Truly, a glorious death.

Nonaka was not the inventor of this method of attack. It

was Flight Sergeant Oda of the 2nd Squadron who had first rammed an adversary. On May 8, 1943, his Hayabusa had taken off with others from a base in New Guinea. Their mission was to defend our convoy making for Madan, a revictualling base on this large island. Oda's formation spotted an enemy bomber, a B-17. If they did not shoot it down, the pilot would report the position of the convoy to his base. A catastrophe. It was therefore essential to bring that B-17 down. Oda attacked it several times, but without success. The little Ki-43 fighter could not long maintain the altitude of the B-17. 'Our convoy is in danger!' thought Oda, and this thought inspired him to charge head on at the enemy, spitting fire. But still the B-17 flew on. Shortly afterwards, Flight Lieutenant Kobayashi, who was leading the formation, saw Oda's Falcon crash into the bomber. His plane ripped a wing of the bomber and the two planes fell in a burst of flame.

What Kagawa had said remained strangely clear in my memory. Certainly this method of attack was the only infallible one. Perhaps the ordinary fighter plane, in case of emergency, had to have recourse to such extreme measures. I could not but admire Flight Sergeant Oda, whose lone action had saved several thousand of our soldiers, for, without it, the convoy would have been destroyed. He had certainly earned his promotion. Nonaka's case was not identical – he was piloting the *Toryu*, which was better armed and capable of maintaining the high altitude of the B-29.

'But,' I said to Furukawa after a long silence, 'they say the Ki-45 Kai has been specially armed to combat the giant bomber. In my opinion, Nonaka should have found some other means of destroying the bomber. Wasn't he carried away by his impetuosity? And you could say the same of Rear Admiral Inokuchi, the commander of the *Musashi*.'

'What?' he snapped aggressively. 'Do you mean to say you have no sympathy with the heroic feelings of the Admiral?'

'None! He was an acknowledged master in the art of manoeuvring a ship. His life was a valuable asset to our Imperial Navy, especially in the present crisis, so it was his duty to survive at all costs. A life is irreplaceable!'

'Rubbish! He fulfilled his duty by writing out the specific improvements that should be carried out in the armament of his battleship.'

'He would have done better to give the General Staff a verbal account of his ideas. It would have been clearer and more detailed.'

'He must have said to himself: "How can I return alive when the ship entrusted to me by His Imperial Majesty has been lost?" '

'If so, his thinking was gravely mistaken. Death leads nowhere!'

'You attach too much importance to life. Suppose the whole world perished, except you yourself. Would you have any desire to live, all alone? If human life has any high purpose at all, it is to communicate with other human beings. This is the source of the principle of *honour*. I believe that life is based on this idea. It is the essence of *Bushido*, as demonstrated by the conduct of the ancient Samurais. Even Europeans fight duels to save their personal honour. A human being who has lost his self-respect through clinging too tenaciously to life is without honour.'

'Let's come back to Rear Admiral Inokuchi. For him, honour must have meant the fulfilment of his duty as a naval officer, that is to say, he should have taken command of another battle-ship and destroyed the maximum possible number of enemy ships, until Destiny dictated the hour of his death. By committing suicide, he was simply running away from his responsibility!'

'Perhaps he was mortally wounded and had not long to live. Besides, for him, his ship was like his own family. He would have wanted to share in the death of his dying child. All the commanders of warships comport themselves in this stoic manner. Can't you understand the heart of a father who does not wish to outlive his loved ones, even for a moment? There are two kinds of life: the life of the beasts, which is governed entirely by instinct, and the life of man, who lives consciously and serves some purpose . . . call it the community, if you like. If man existed merely for the sake of existing, what a burden life would be! A sense of life and death is not taught to us by reason. Besides, reason is not always the ally of the heart. . . . '

Abruptly, he stopped speaking. No doubt he was put off by my absent air. Indeed, I was listening with only half an ear. The familiar black speck, dancing in front of my eyes, that symbol of death, was tormenting me. I was in anguish. For some time, when I was not actually in the air flying, I had shown myself to be a sceptic on the subject of voluntary death. My vehemence on the subject had earned me the nick-name: 'Aspirant Philosopher'. A philosopher indeed! I was nothing, in reality, but a pilot, well trained and earnest, and my country had need of such men. When it was a question of the heroic exploits of Flight Sergeants Oda and Nonaka, I made no comment. I had doubts about the spirit of *Bushido* – that principle that negates death. But in the depths of my heart perhaps the presentiment was already forming that I too, in the end, would act as they had done. I trusted my impulses. Probably my ardent desire to live drew nourishment from this very premonition, which urged me to underline the importance of life.

I cast an envious glance at my relaxed and tranquil companions. What indeed was the use of being a philosopher, musing on the subject of life and death, when you were in the midst of an aerial battle?

I stood up abruptly, then asked Imamura for permission to raise the blind slightly. I wanted a final glimpse of Mount Fuji. 'We're not at a station. All right, then, but only for a minute, eh?' he replied. I hastily raised the blind. Alas! Clouds obscured the sky and visibility was almost nil. I sat down again, resigned. Furukawa had already moved and was sitting beside another of our comrades.

It was three in the morning. The train was standing at a station. Some policemen came into our compartment. Almost everyone was fast asleep. As I was awake, one of the police came towards me and told me he was going to refill our water bottles with hot green tea. I nodded and asked him what station we were in. 'Nagoya, Cadet Pilot!' he said. Nagoya, my home town! My family were no longer there, they were now staying in the country, to the east of this large industrial and commercial city. I saw again my sisters waving to me, at the end of the same platform, six months ago. Why is it we only realise the depths of our affection when faced with a final separation?

And then, I remembered a childhood sweetheart: the little girl I had been in love with, without knowing what love was. Was she still living in this city? Recollections of the distant past bathed me in happiness, like a caress. I leaned my forehead against the blind in the vague hopes of seeing the city, though it must be in total darkness. The blind was impenetrable. As the train started with a jolt, I said to this invisible city: 'Goodbye, so sorry I shall not see you again . . . '

After travelling for twenty-four hours, we arrived at the base of Ozuki, about eight miles east of Shimonoseki. Properly speaking, it is not in Kyushu; nevertheless, the 4th Squadron was responsible for the defence of the northern skies over this island, which includes the two large industrial towns of Yahata and Kokura. Backed by mountains, the aerodrome looked out over the sea. The terrain had formerly been a quarry. The icy winter wind off the sea howled, bellowed, whistled and rattled. Now and again, it raised minor tornadoes. We could dimly see the outline of Kyushu, black and indented. On the sea, there was not a single fishing boat, for it was mortally dangerous; testing fire was carried out in the direction of the sea before the planes took off to confront the B-29s and there was not time to warn the fishing boats each time. Enemy air raids had become so frequent now that our pilots had to be ready day and night.

The airfield was enormous: there were two concrete runways, one at the foot of a mountain and the other at the edge of the sea. Our air strength was made up of two squadrons, the fighters and the reconnaissance planes. The twenty-seven cadet pilots belonged to the fighter squadron, which used the airstrip along the seashore. In October, at Utsunomiya Flying School, each of us had been asked to choose: fighter, bomber or reconnaissance plane. I had hesitated for a moment as I filled out the questionnaire. I had said to myself: 'If I opt for bombers, I might possibly be sent to the base at Hamamatsu, near Shizuoka. That would give me a chance to see my old high school again. However, I do not feel the least desire to be a bomber pilot. That cumbersome machine is an easy prey for enemy fighters. Besides, the pilot is responsible for the lives of the other men in his crew, whereas the fighter pilot has the advantage of single-handed combat, man to man. I can't imagine anything more splendid for a fighting pilot.' After some hours of reflection, I chose the fighter. All the cadets had made the same choice. Squadron Leader Watanabe declared: 'Our school has no pilots to send to the bomber or reconnaissance squadrons! Too bad, but I respect each man's choice.'

Our squadron had at its disposal planes of Type 97, Ki-27 and *Toryu*. The majority were of the last type. These twin-engined two-seaters served principally as survey planes over

75

the terrains in China and the Marianas where the B-29s were based. They played a vital role in the defence of the Nipponese Archipelago. Their engines were 1,055-horsepower. They were armed with one 37-mm. cannon, two 20-mm. cannon and two 12.7-mm. machine guns. The 7.7-mm. machine gun, formerly used as a rear gun, had been removed as it had proved to be quite useless against the American Superfortresses. This plane flew at a speed of 340 miles per hour and had a range of approximately 1,250 miles. First put into service in September, 1942, it had been used both as fighter and bomber, particularly in the New Guinea zone. Since the emergence of the B-29, its fire-power had been improved, thus rendering it far more effective. Camouflaged in dark green patched with grey, its silhouette made me think of a huge lizard, while the recon-naissance plane type 100 (Ki-46), with its natural silvery duralumin colour, uncamouflaged, made me think of a brittle snake. That lumbering lizard, the *Toryu*, proved to be virtually impotent when faced with the American light fighters. In October, forty Grumman F-6-Fs had attacked our naval air base at Formosa. Ten *Toryus* of the 3rd Advanced Training Corps had taken off to intercept the enemy formation. When they reached their maximum altitude in formation, the enemy aircraft dived down on them from a height of over 6,000 feet above their heads. Difficult to manoeuvre, our planes were unable to save themselves from this high-angle attack. They were like lizards pounced upon by birds of prey. Within a few minutes, all ten *Toryus* had gone down. A disastrous experience.

The fighter squadron was divided into three flights, and the *Toryus* bore white, red or yellow markings according to their flight number. To our great regret, we were not assigned to these fighting arms, but had to content ourselves with perfecting our flying technique in fighters of Type 97.

This fighter had first seen service in December, 1933, after which it was immediately produced in great numbers and re-mained in service up until the end of the war. Its manoeuvrability had outclassed that of all its rivals during the Sino-Japanese conflict. This 785-horsepower single-seater had, in its time, been considered a revolutionary design. Its speed, at an altitude of 11,400 feet, was about 295 miles per hour. It had a range of nearly 400 miles and was armed with two 7.7-mm. machine guns. By the end of 1942, 3,386 of these planes had been built,

76

with various modifications to the original design. It never went out of production, even when the Hayabusa appeared in 1941.

Even during the first phase of the Pacific war, these planes continued to demonstrate their patent superiority over the enemy fighters. Their dazzling victories were in part due to their extreme manoeuvrability, which enabled them to gain altitude rapidly on their backs, or undertake a series of tight turns so as to stick close to the adversary. Nobody would have denied that the Ki-27 was one of the masterpieces of world aviation, but, at a time when our army was immensely proud of this aircraft, the world powers, led by the U.S.A., the U.S.S.R. and Germany, had begun to attach importance to heavy fighters with more powerful weapons. In this field, Germany was unbeatable with her Bf-209. Nevertheless, three great powers, Britain, Italy and Japan, continued to prefer light fighters.

Why this preference? I suppose in Japan it had its source in the traditional spirit of the Samurais. Their greatest honour was to challenge a renowned champion to single combat. They had boundless contempt for the warrior who relied upon superiority of numbers to defeat an illustrious captain. A Samurai, confident of his fighting abilities and mounted on a horse skilled in all sorts of acrobatics, asked for nothing more as long as he was fighting. Our Ki-27 pilots, imbued with the Samurai spirit, had succeeded in smashing the enemy fighters in China, in a manner that was in keeping with the ancient tradition. This kind of combat suited the talents of the Ki-27, but were such tactics valid in modern warfare? There were doubts. The acid test: the Ki-27s had not been able to catch the B-25s of the Doolittle Flight in April, due to their lack of speed. They had a fixed undercarriage. For a long time pilots of the Imperial Army Air Fleet had been crying out for new fighters designed to mitigate the shortcomings of the Ki-27.

Certainly, as a trainer plane, it was easy to fly, though the use of A-Go fuel for training purposes meant the pilot had to pay the very closest attention at all times. We were very keen on the firing practice which we now carried out during lulls between American raids.

During the early days of December, we had one evening's leave. Flying Officer Imamura had asked the commander-in-chief to grant a day of rest to his twenty-seven cadets, who had never had a day's leave since joining up.

That day, according to reports from several Ki-46s, the B-29s based in China were not expected to raid Kyushu. Everybody jumped for joy. How long we had been waiting for this! Cadet Pilot Toda exulted at the idea of seeing his fiancée, who lived in Shimonoseki. He came from a small town in northern Kyushu, and would have liked to visit his home too, but we were not allowed to travel farther afield than Shimonoseki. We had only six hours off, from 1600 hours to 2200. As for me, on thinking it over, I gave up the idea of going to Shimonoseki, since I knew no one there. Besides, there would not be much to see, and all the cinemas and theatres were closed. If I went into town, it would only be to go to bed with a common prostitute in the brothel reserved for officers. Rather than waste my time thus, I preferred to rest. Several of my comrades were of the same opinion. Unconsciously, I had become accustomed to life in the large community of the barracks, a life governed by a rigorous discipline, and I was beginning to feel that it was from habit and routine, rather than change, that one drew one's greatest pleasures.

While we were dozing on our beds, a soldier of the Aviation Service Corps came to announce the beginning of the recreation period. A theatrical troupe were to act on an improvised stage in a corner of a hangar. At the insistence of my companions, I finally got up and went with them. Soldiers, too long deprived of pleasure and entertainment, were running towards the hangar. The curtain had already been raised and the play, a martially-inspired piece, was in progress. A mother had lost four of her sons in the war; she was saying to her fifth son, who was about to leave for the front: 'Your four brothers have sacrificed their lives for their country. I am happy, and I am proud of them. Make sure you, too, die gloriously! If you come back, I will not allow you to enter the house!'

These exaggerated words rang horribly false. Angered by the mother's harshness, I felt like shouting: 'Stop it! Have you no compassion for the feelings of Yamada's mother? We fighting men are cogs in an infernal machine called war, it forces us to be inhuman monsters, isn't that bad enough? Must you too cease to be a human being? Death is the logical consequence of war, and it is pitiless. Do not trifle with it. Your futile words only sadden your son, whereas your tears would give him courage. For us, it would be cowardly to

78

tremble, to weep, to pray. But you, you have the right to weep tender tears. Weep, then!' I hated the actress who was playing the role of the mother. She was, in any case, a ham. It was only a theatrical show, and yet I was carried away with fury, for I could imagine my mother dissolving in tears as she read the announcement of my death in action. The contrast was unbearable.

Ten minutes later, I left the hangar alone and went back to our billet. The storm of applause which I had left behind me cut me off still more absolutely from the outside world. I stopped in front of the half-opened door to one of the officers' rooms: I glimpsed an officer sitting there writing. He was wearing a flying suit. It was Flying Officer Fujisaki, who was said to be an ex-student from the Imperial University of Tokyo. He was, therefore, a forerunner of mine, for in October I too had been admitted to the French Literature Department of this university. As the number of students applying for the Faculty of Letters had not reached full quota, as they did in the years before the war, I had been admitted without examinations. Amongst my friends, Oshima had registered at the Law Faculty of the Imperial University of Tokyo, Suzuki at the Imperial University of Tohoku (at Sendai), and Saga at the Medical Faculty in Nagasaki.

I felt a sympathy for Fujisaki, although I had never spoken to him. Behind his high forehead, one guessed, there was intelligence and phlegm. I knocked at the door, then asked if I might come in. He raised his eyes and said crossly: 'Come in!' I walked up to his desk and said loudly: 'Cadet Pilot Nagatsuka! I am a student at the Imperial University of Tokyo, like you, Flying Officer!'

'Well, well,' he said. 'What a pleasant surprise to find a student from my university in this squadron! I was in the first intake of *tokusos*. I was studying at the Faculty of Law – and you?'

His attitude changed. Instead of being a superior officer, he was once more a fellow-student. He invited me to sit down. 'You stayed behind, then?' he asked. 'Yes,' I replied. 'I just watched the play in the hangar. It was awful! The death of a fighting man . . .'

I stopped. I would have liked to confess all my thoughts, but did not dare. Despite the kindness he was showing me, he was still my superior officer. In the army, rank is all-important. Noticing my hesitation, he took me up:

'Ah, well! I can guess what you're going to say. That's enough. We students from high schools have read too many books on philosophy. We have acquired the habit of thinking that scepticism leads to truth. But when you're engaged in a dogfight in the air, all ideas of death, life, feeling, are nothing but metaphysics, they contain nothing positive. An aerial battle is beyond philosophy, it is a critical point, the simple projection of temperament over ideas. You are still weighed down with metaphysical meditations because you have not yet experienced the reality of combat. In a few days, you cadets will have to confront the B-29s. You will undergo an initiatory flight on board Ki-45 Kais piloted by your seniors. Would you like to fly in my plane?'

I shall never forget his expression – it was dynamic, full of strength, resolution, lucidity, and apparently without care or worry. I felt the fullest confidence in him and accepted the offer unhesitatingly.

'Good,' he said quietly. 'I will talk to the commander about it. You understand, of course, that we shall run the risk of being shot down by the enemy. They are extraordinarily well armed, you know. But one must take risks in order to succeed in anything. Afterwards, you will be capable of shooting down a B-29 yourself.'

I will make no bones about it – this first sortie terrified me. It takes several sorties to get oneself acclimatised to war. And there is a vast gulf between acclimatisation and over-confidence. Disdain for one's foe leads to a fatal lack of caution.

I chatted with him for over an hour, about a variety of things. This fruitful conversation stimulated me, and made me realise the outstanding personality of my interlocutor. Flying Officer Fujisaki, who was to die on a suicide-mission at sea near Okinawa in May, 1945, had been transferred to the base at Ozuki in June, 1944. Later, he brought down three Superfortresses over northern Kyushu.

To paint an exact portrait of this officer, it is necessary to recall an incident in which he was personally involved soon after he arrived at the base.

When an air raid alert sounded, it was the practice for one pilot to take off and fly over the town in the vicinity of the base. Over Shimonoseki, he would execute a loop-the-loop, which was the signal for aviators on leave in the town to return to base immediately.

A few days after his arrival at Ozuki, Fujisaki was given this mission. He was rather disappointed by this, as he had never yet engaged in aerial combat, and felt he was missing the chance now. Moreover, being sent on this errand signified to the other pilots that he was not yet fully qualified.

Now, when he returned to the airfield, after accomplishing his mission, he watched a spectacle that was to make a deep impression on him: Flight Sergeant Nonaka, who was amongst those pilots recalled from Shimonoseki, had leapt into his Ki-45 Kai without even bothering to put on his flying suit, and taken off precipitately. Fujisaki followed Nonaka's aerial evolutions for about half an hour, and then saw his plane hurl itself, from below, against the left wing of a B-29 at an altitude of about 25,000 feet. The two machines, belching flame, hurtled down like meteors. This prodigal feat held him spellbound. But he was cool enough to calculate: 'This method of attack, even though you risk almost certain death, is not as easy as it looks.'

After my conversation with him, I went back to our room, where I found most of my companions back from leave. Since there were few places of entertainment open, they had had to make do with drifting around the deserted streets of Shimonoseki, and so, disappointed, had come back to barracks three hours early. 'All we did was wear ourselves out,' somebody complained. Just before 2200 hours, Toda came in. A minute later, the gate was closed. Unexpectedly, Toda seemed dejected and exuded an infinite sorrow. 'What's the matter?' said Furukawa, 'Didn't you have a splendid evening with your fiancée? You're pulling a long face!' Toda shrugged his shoulders wearily, then replied: 'It's nothing. But do I really look depressed?' He sat still for a moment, then undressed.

After lights-out, I heard Toda talking quietly to Furukawa. His voice was just a harsh, hoarse whisper.

'Oof!' he grumbled. 'I behaved like a fool this evening. I'm sorry I went to see my fiancée, and the worst of it is, I went to bed with her. I couldn't resist.'

'So what!' said Furukawa. 'We all give way to instinct at times. In any case, it's too late to worry about it. It's done.'

'Ah, but I should have broken off our engagement, that's what I went to Shimonoseki for. You see, I know we won't

6   81

come out of this war alive. But when I was face to face with her, I hadn't the courage. I behaved like a coward.'

'You're too sensitive about it. But you should marry her as soon as possible, in case there's a child. . . . You could ask for compassionate leave . . .'

'No! That's not the problem . . . you see . . .'

Toda hesitated a moment, as if he wanted to make sure the other men were asleep.

Curiosity is a mean vice, but in spite of myself, my ears were flapping!

'I have a confession to make,' he went on in a rather embarrassed voice. 'She had her period . . . well . . . she's not a virgin anymore, because I. . . . Excuse me for being so indiscreet, but I am full of remorse! It will be impossible for her to marry another man as a chaste woman . . . and I went to bed with her knowing I couldn't marry her, because I am bound to be killed. How can I atone for this sin? Marriage is out of the question. Pilots' wives are always destined to be widows. I love her as much as ever, but I should have broken off our engagement as soon as I joined up. . . .'

'I think you're taking your responsibilities too seriously. You shouldn't be a slave to tradition.'

'That's the least of my worries! Besides, I don't believe in that kind of superstition. . . .'

The most dangerous thing for a pilot, when flying or when involved in an air battle, is to be a prey to worry. Flying Officer Fujisaki had advised me to see a specialist about the injury to my leg. Toda's problems could seriously disturb his peace of mind. It was my duty to intervene, so I said to them straight out: 'Sssh! You're keeping me awake!' and they stopped whispering.

Next day, after much hesitation, I went to the infirmary. If the senior physician ordered me to spend several days in bed, or undergo an operation, it would delay my training programme. However, after a careful examination, the doctor diagnosed a bruising of the nerves, which was not serious. But my leg was still insensitive to touch and to changes in temperature. It was very odd! 'There is no specific treatment,' he concluded. 'If it doesn't prevent your flying, don't worry about it. It will heal itself in time.'

Just as I was leaving the consulting room, feeling somewhat

relieved, I saw one of the cadet pilots rushing towards the infirmary.

'Cadet Pilot Toda's plane has just crashed into a mountain. It's in flames!' he burst out.

A shiver of terror and anguish shook me: the prediction made by Komorizono had been verified in the most sinister fashion. I ran to the far end of the airfield and saw the plane, which was just burning itself out in the distance. A red glow looked like the peaceful lamp on a fishing boat. According to several witnesses, Toda's plane had lost speed and fallen during gunnery practice against a floating target. After diving down over the sea, with his guns blazing, he had climbed steeply over the shore line. A second later, they had seen his plane side-slip and then go into a tail spin. Had his angle of ascent been too steep? If his engine had been fed by normal fuel, there would have been no difficulty in avoiding loss of speed, but with the A-Go fuel used in the Ki-27, there was nothing one could do. The accident was due to that damnable fuel. Or else Toda had been obsessed with morbid presentiments during his flight. A moment's distraction or inattention, provoked by memories of his love-making with his fiancée, would have sufficed. Of course, one would never know the real cause of the accident.

Just before 1500 hours, the Service Corps personnel removed the body. Death was now part of our routine: we had seen pilots shot down, and others who had died from bullet wounds immediately after landing. Mechanically, we gathered together Toda's belongings to send them back to his family. Someone found the photograph of a young girl between two pages of his diary. His fiancée, no doubt, since Toda had no sister. She was a pretty girl with an oval face, and her whole soul was reflected in a truly feminine smile. Her clear eyes expressed a rather childish candour. I did not even know the girl, yet I could not help wondering what would become of her.

Certainly, a pilot's death could be caused by a mere caprice of fate. But, for myself, I would do everything I could to minimise the risk, and, if I could not avoid death, I would prefer to choose the hour and the manner of it, as Oda and Nonaka had done, provided it would be of service to my country.

That same evening, I received a letter from my university. I was asked to send them, urgently, a military certificate, in accordance with the 'deferment of studies' formalities. I went to Squadron Leader Takahashi's office to ask him to stamp my documents. The commander, who had just returned from a night flight, was deliberating with the leaders of the three flights. Absorbed in their discussion, they paid no attention to me. The interview, which looked as if it would be a long one, was concerned with the reorganisation of the three attack groups. Should I wait or go away? I hesitated, and as I was about to leave discreetly, the commander said: 'You may remain. Wait for me.' Standing rigidly at attention, I waited in a corner of the office.

Flight Lieutenant Sanaka, leader of the 2nd Flight, spoke: 'We must remember that we have fewer and fewer Ki-45 Kais available, sir.'

'Of course,' replied Takahashi, 'you're right in a way, but think: the speed and the weapons of the Ki-27 don't measure up to those of the B-29.'

'Excuse me, sir,' replied Sanaka, with a great show of modesty, 'but I think it is indispensable to use all the aircraft at our disposal, so as to wipe out the greatest possible number of these American bombers.'

'And the pilots? They are not yet sufficiently trained.'

'But what counts is neither the skill of the pilots nor the quality of the planes. The important thing is the spirit and morale of our men.'

'That is mere sentiment,' observed Flight Lieutenant Togashi, leader of the 3rd Flight.

These two officers came from the Army Flying School. Their characters were diametrically opposed. A native of Kyushu, and proud of being a true Japanese, Flight Lieutenant Sanaka was something of a fanatic; at times, his passion reached an extraordinary pitch of frenzy. Togashi, on the other hand, was always calm and resolute; his black sparkling eyes expressed an inflexible will; the brisk manner in which he returned subordinates' salutes was typical of the man, and the pilots in his flight took a delight in imitating him. His incredible dexterity in getting the Ki-45 Kai off the ground is beyond any words of mine to praise. In spite of the weight of the machine, he would take off in the shortest possible distance . . . which was extremely important when going to intercept enemy aircraft, for the essential thing was to be away, gain altitude and get into formation very fast. Togashi, who knew the performance of the Ki-45 Kai like the back of his hand, elevated the nose of his plane to a climbing angle that was just within the stalling margin. He went up like a rocket. It was astonishing, marvellous. He handled this heavy fighter, which was so difficult to fly, as if it were a toy. And he had shot down more than ten Superfortresses!

'Bah!' retorted Sanaka. 'Logic is the last thing you can apply to battle.'

'Right!' the commander finally concluded. 'We shall organise an attack flight with cadet pilots. In the last few days, the B-29s have been flying over Kyushu at a much lower altitude. The Ki-27s will be able to attack them at sixteen thousand feet. To begin with, the cadets will go out on initiation flights on the Ki-45 Kais. Then they will sortie in the Ki-27.'

The flight leaders left the office quickly, without looking at me. I stepped forward and explained the object of my visit to the commanding officer. He glanced through my papers in the half-light, for all lights on the base were shaded. His look, gentle enough as a rule, suddenly transfixed me with a shaft of ice.

'Listen,' he said gruffly, 'do you seriously believe you'll be able to take up your studies again?'

What answer could I give? Of course, there was no certainty that I would survive. I could not count on anyone, not even the Almighty, to protect me from death. And I had seen the cruelty, the atrocity of war: what a spectacle when the *Toryus* limped home, wounded, bleeding, at their last gasp! Some of the pilots breathed their last as they were being carried to the infirmary. Whenever I saw such scenes, I reacted, like all timid ditherers, by vowing that I would not give a thought to my own life during combat. No, there was not the slightest chance that one day I would resume my student life. Nevertheless, I was very keen to remain on the register of the faculty. What inward contradictions!

'No, sir,' I said after thinking it over. 'But it's only a formality. I swear to you it will not in any way deter me from willingly risking my life.'

'Among the ancient Samurais, the warrior who threw away the sheath of his sword before a fight was looked upon as already vanquished: after his death, he would have no need of a sword sheath! The Samurai who was confident never threw

85

away his sheath, because he knew he would need it after he had won the victory. Now, where do you stand?'

His tone was sharp, although his voice seemed entirely devoid of feeling. He did not press the point any further, but stamped my papers mechanically and handed them back to me, saying: 'We have decided to send the cadet pilots out against the B-29s, you know. I hope these papers will not undermine your courage and make you spend your time longing for your literary studies. . . . '

He was right. Literature encourages humanism, whereas combat has the sole aim of killing, consequently eliminating all humane feeling. On the evidence, literature and war are at opposite poles. I made an unshakable decision: to abandon all idea of returning to the faculty and dedicate myself absolutely to my patriotic duty.

The great vault of the blue, mysterious sky stretched all about us. Not a cloud: visibility excellent. The indentations of the coast stood out sharply against the emerald-green depths of the sea. As far as I could judge, the 2nd Attack Flight was maintaining an altitude of 19,500 feet. The formation was composed of Ki-45 Kais. Sitting in the machine-gunner's place, I could not see the altimeter, so I could only guess the altitude approximately. Since the Ki-45 Kai had long ago got rid of its 7.7-mm. machine gun, the four cadet pilots who were going out on this initiatory flight were installed in the gunners' seats. We had been ordered to jump by parachute in case of emergency, but Flying Officer Fujisaki had said to me: 'Today, as I have a pilot behind me who is lacking in experience, I shall not jump until you've had time to get out, if the plane happens to get hit. In any case, a Japanese pilot should not abandon a burning plane, it would endanger houses and people on the ground. In such a case, I would do my best to take the plane out over the sea, or a mountainous region before I jumped. Anyway, whatever happens, keep calm.'

I had the utmost confidence in him, so much so that I had put my parachute aside, thinking I might be better off without it, as it was an encumbrance. In spite of the high altitude, we were able to breathe easily, thanks to the oxygen respirators.

The 2nd Flight kept watch on the movements of the B-29s to the southwest of Yahata. The enemy tactic consisted of spreading his formation over the Goto Islands and then making for northern Kyushu. After the bombing, the planes would regroup over the Goto Islands and then return to their bases in China.

I felt completely different from the way I had felt during training flights. I was about to witness a real battle. I kept my eyes wide open and looked about me on all sides. Suddenly, I saw Flying Officer Fujisaki pointing to ten o'clock. Down there, several small dots were glinting in the sun like swords. The Flying Fortresses! The enemy were flying at an altitude of about 23,000 feet. Our patrol leader waggled his wings. This was the signal for the formation to spread out. Fujisaki gained height. Seen from behind, his massive silhouette remained unruffled, but his face must have worn the expression of a fighter pilot – energetic and full of a fierce will.

We were closing in on our adversaries. The four pilots, each carrying a cadet in the gunner's seat, had been ordered not to approach the enemy too closely. When we were at a distance of some 3,000 feet, Fujisaki lost height a little. In spite of orders, he intended to attack from close to, that was certain. The 37-mm. gun on the Ki-45 Kai, placed in the middle of the fuselage, was not very practical in reality, since there was an interval of one to two seconds between each burst of fire. This interfered with one's aim. Besides, this cannon had only sixteen projectiles. The pilot was forced to rely mainly on his two 20-mm. cannon. Fixed to the floor of the fuselage, they were pointed upward at an angle of twenty degrees. For all these reasons, the fighter pilot had to attack the mammoth bomber from below. The B-29 had hardly any blind spots thanks to its numerous defence turrets. Its maximum speed of 370 miles per hour was superior to that of the Ki-45 Kai, which made it difficult for the latter to catch up with the bomber from behind, in order to attack.

At a distance of 1,000 feet, I had a clear view of this famous bomber for the first time. It was like some fabulous flying castle. Its elegant, uncamouflaged fuselage made me think of a monstrous flying fish. What imposing fins, what a rudder! The most disquieting thing about it was those six domes: two gun turrets on its back and four defence turrets operated by remote control – two at the back, one above, one below; and two in front, one on top and one in the waist of the plane. Each of these firing points was armed with two 12.7-mm. machine guns. Each gun was loaded with 1,000 bullets. It possessed, moreover, a tail turret with two 12.7-mm. machine guns and a 20-mm. cannon. The four engines developed 8,800 horsepower. The white star that stood out against a black background seemed to me like a challenge. It was the mark of the enemy. Four months ago, in a dream, I had seen an American bomber flying over Japan. This dream ceased to be a memory and became a reality: I was living it. The crimson face of the pilot remained present in my mind. I was at the very peak of excitement.

Suddenly, the two forward turrets of the B-29 opened fire. I saw tracer bullets racing towards our plane. Japanese pilots called them *ice-candies*. These ice-candies instantly melted to port and starboard, like little fireworks whose colour and brilliance lasted but a moment. Strange! I was not in the least afraid. But this absence of fear did not mean I was numb or insensitive. On the contrary, I was absolutely fascinated to see what counterstroke Fujisaki would devise. At 800 feet, he launched the ice-candies from his own 12.7-mm. machine guns. They also vanished in the void . . . 600 feet . . . 450 feet . . . Fujisaki's aircraft was rapidly approaching the Superfortress from below. The huge wing of the bomber seemed to hang over us. An attack of this sort seemed to me vain in the face of the enormous bulk of the B-29 . . . 300 feet . . . Fujisaki kept up a steady stream of projectiles from his two cannon, aiming at the nose of the bomber. To shoot down a B-29, it was more efficacious to hit the pilot and the co-pilot than the petrol tanks, which were automatically self-sealing. I saw Fujisaki's ice-candies glance off the pilot's seat; our adversary went into a side-slip to elude the attack. In spite of its cumbersome appearance, the B-29 was not lacking in agility. I must admit, I was astonished. Fujisaki promptly broke off the fight by executing an Immelmann. The ice-candies pursued us. Then I felt a jolt as some of them pierced the edge of the port wing. It was not serious. Our enemy flew cheerfully on. Really, there was a cheeky air about him!

Fujisaki gained altitude to level out. The B-29 was ahead of us, at four o'clock. There was a difference of about 1,500 feet in our altitudes. Fujisaki had the audacity to go into a dive, and then, flying some 600 feet over the Fortress, he loosed a number of projectiles from his 20-mm. cannon. The multi-coloured traces of the bullets crossed and criss-crossed vertically without reaching their target. Fujisaki side-slipped again to make his getaway.

He had no time to turn round and look at me, but I could imagine his face contorted by tension and irritation all the time. Our enemy flew away towards the sky over Kokura, already starred with anti-aircraft fire. Fujisaki gave up the chase and changed direction, intending to follow another B-29. I followed with my eyes the American who had just escaped us and saw two *Toryus* attack him from beneath, on either side. The Superfortress spat white smoke, turned north and fled towards the sea. Perhaps they could bring it down?

Fujisaki latched on to another Flying Fortress, from below on the starboard side, as he had with the previous one. He renewed his attack several times but without success. Plumes of smoke from the ice-candies of both planes mingled in the sky. The intense fire-power of the B-29 kept the Ki-45 Kai at a distance. After twenty minutes' skirmishing, Fujisaki had exhausted his ammunition. He raised his left hand to warn me that we were about to go down. We could no longer see either the B-29 or the ack-ack barrage over Kokura and Yahata. Several black columns of smoke rose from these two towns: the bombers must have passed that way. . . .

All around me, the sky was serene, as if nothing had happened, but in my mind the image of the criss-crossing ice-candies remained vivid. From time to time, our plane was lightly brushed by rags of cloud, and I suffered the illusion that they were tracer bullets.

Fujisaki lost altitude rapidly. I took off my oxygen mask. The cold air clenched the muscles of my face, for the gunner's seat had no windshield, so as to allow free movement of the weapon. I breathed in deeply through nose and mouth, as though I had just returned to my natural element. The air tasted quite delicious to me, like some unknown taste that revives you with its fresh savour. A number of ambulances were lined up along the airstrip at the base. Had some of our pilots been wounded? The *Toryus* landed, one after the other. The ambulances did not move. Apparently, there were no casualties. Fujisaki made his landing approach. He lowered the flaps. We could see the waves now, more and more sharply defined on the surface of the water.

After landing, Fujisaki and I went directly to the briefing room. We stood at attention and saluted Commander Taka-hashi. Then Fujisaki reported: 'Flying Officer Fujisaki and

Cadet Pilot Nagatsuka,' he said loudly. 'Result: nil. That is all.'

A certain pallor betrayed his rage and frustration. The squadron leader acknowledged the report with a brief nod of the head and said nothing. Other pilots were standing at attention behind us. We went and sat under the awning.

'Damn!' snapped Fujisaki. 'I am still not good enough.'

The presence of a novice in his plane had prevented his approaching the enemy too closely, and I knew it. Without me, he would probably have shot down a B-29, but Fujisaki never sought to excuse himself. In the army, excuses are merely a sign of cowardice and lack of will; they are not to be tolerated.

Ten minutes later, the leader of the 2nd Flight landed. He was the last. The white circle painted in the middle of the fuselage was his distinctive mark as leader. Flight Lieutenant Sanaka went into the briefing room and gave a brief report:

'Sir,' he said, 'the Second Flight has completed its mission. I shot one bomber down. That is all.'

The blood had mounted to his face but his expression was the same as usual. Several bullet holes were visible in the fuselage and rudder of his plane. Altogether, two bombers had been brought down. Before breaking ranks, Sanaka said to his pilots: 'When fighting a bomber, the vital thing is to get in as close as possible, whereas when you're in a dogfight with another fighter, the main thing is to spot it as soon as possible. Don't forget that! Dismissed!'

I walked back to barracks beside Fujisaki. He did not speak. Not the least sign of fatigue showed in his face. He strode along, staring straight in front of him and even forgetting to return the mechanics' salutes. His whole body expressed bitterness, frustration, wrath. In front of the officers' room, I said: 'Permit me to leave you, sir.' Grinding his teeth and clenching his fists because he had not brought down a B-29, he looked me in the eyes and said simply: 'Right. Now you understand what an air battle is. I hope so, anyway. In a few days, it will be your turn to go through it. I shall be in command of the cadet pilots' flight. Go on then, and good luck!'

In the trainees' room, I found a postcard from Saga, a schoolfellow, on my table. He had been studying medicine at Nagasaki since October. This city in western Kyushu was a military port and a great centre for ship building and naval

90

repairs. When a criminal American pilot dropped an atom bomb on August 9, 1945, there were 85,000 victims, and my comrade must have been amongst them. This unique bomb, frightful and inhuman, did not even leave corpses. Inhabitants who found themselves within a perimeter of 3,000 yards of the epicentre were affected by radiation and died like the people of Hiroshima, where the Americans had dropped the first atomic bomb three days earlier.

Saga's characteristic writing, very clear, slender and neat, brought back memories of the past.

'My dear Nagatsuka,' he wrote, 'I hope that you are applying yourself diligently to your military training. I often think of you, as you must be flying over this city. I am devoting myself to learning German, rather than medicine, as this language is essential to a study of medical science. I hope soon to be able to read the works of Kant. In our human society, ambition and self-interest are at the root of many betrayals, whereas knowledge never betrays those who woo her. I am happy that I am able to indulge my passion for her. . . .'

Knowledge never betrays those who woo her. . . . How true! Nevertheless, I was in no mood to share his passion for knowledge. It no longer had a place in my universe, it had become a stranger to me. Now that I had actually taken part in an aerial combat, I became aware of the impenetrable barrier that separated me once and for all from my student life. An abyss had opened between my way of thinking and that of my ex-companions from the high school. Not without regret, I felt that my feelings and my attitude to life cut me off completely from them. My duty consisted in protecting them at the risk of my own life, and in allowing them to devote their time to studies without worrying. My conclusion was totally unambiguous: *I am a pilot, uniquely dedicated to war.* It was no good hankering after the past. For me, Cicero's declaration was apt: Philosophy is nothing but a preparation for death. Since I would soon be involved in the reality of war in the air, the one thing that mattered to me was to acquire an indifference to death. Nostalgia would be cowardly and, in any case, futile. Only the present exists for a pilot. Farewell, past!

Around me, my comrades were talking very eagerly about the battles they had just witnessed. I put Saga's postcard in my drawer without re-reading it, and wrote a note about my first experience of air battle. For the Ki-45 Kai, the best method of attacking the B-29 was still to appoach from below, either on the port or starboard side. All our pilots fired 12.7-mm. tracer bullets so as to adjust the range of their fire before pressing the button of their 20-mm. machine guns. Even so, it was difficult to maintain correct aim because of the climbing angle of the plane. I wondered whether it might not be more effective to fire the machine guns straightaway, using the sights on them rather than the 12.7-mm. gun to adjust the aim. And perhaps it would be preferable to aim at the engine and the wings instead of at the pilots: 20-mm. bullets exploding in the wings might eventually wrench them off. But, alas! The Ki-27 was only armed with two 7.7-mm. machine guns and the bullets did not explode, they simply penetrated. From a Ki-27, therefore, there was no other possibility but to aim at the pilots of the B-29.

I jotted down these reflections which had crossed my mind during the battle. I then read through several pages of the diary which I wrote up almost every evening. Naturally, this was a personal diary, very different from the one we had been obliged to keep, and to present to the flight leader at the flying school every week. Since being assigned to the 4th Squadron, we no longer had to keep this 'official' log, which left us free to consign our observations to our private journals. Nevertheless, I soon realised that even in these personal memoirs, I simply dared not express myself openly and honestly. For example, one day I had written: 'My dearest wish is to die in the air after having shot down the greatest possible number of enemy planes.' I wanted to make a show of sublime heroism, stoic resignation, but . . . for whose benefit? My family's? My ex-comrades from the high school? What vanity! Why hadn't I opened my heart in all honesty and written: 'I want to live at all costs till the war comes to an end'? For I had never ceased to nourish this secret and confused hope of returning alive. Another example: I knew it was absolutely impossible to bring down a B-29 with the 7.7-mm. machine guns on the Ki-27. Yet I had written in my diary: 'It is a pilot's duty to do the impossible. I vow that I will shoot down the B-29s, even though the Ki-27 leaves much to be desired in this respect. I must remain loyal to the military spirit right up to the end.' Hypocrisy and self-flattery! I was ashamed. My only excuse was that I could not write down my true thoughts because I knew that these private memoirs would be read after my death, which would doubtless occur quite soon. Indeed, I considered them as a sort of testament, which I was keeping for my nearest and dearest, and so they contained only half-sincerities, carefully embroidered. My true sentiments, my premonitions, were in any case formed at depths where my conscious mind could not penetrate.

Next evening, I went to see Flying Officer Fujisaki in the officers' sitting room. As always, he received me smilingly and asked me to sit down. I hesitated, as I did not want to unveil my thoughts in front of the other officers. He guessed the reason for my hesitation and at once suggested we should go out. As soon as we were outside, he said: 'In twenty minutes, I have to take part in the night flying training. We haven't much time to chat. Shall we go to the mess? There won't be anybody there at this hour.' I accepted immediately.

He sat down in a corner and looked at me as if to say: 'What is he going through?' I remained standing in front of him, since I could not sit down without his express permission.

'Sir,' I said to him after a moment's thought, 'I understand how difficult it is to bring down these colossal and almost invulnerable bombers, even with heavy fighters. Now, isn't it absurd to attack them with the Ki-27s, which have only two 7.7-mm. machine guns? Their non-explosive bullets are hopelessly inadequate. I know that an iron will is essential to a pilot, but that alone is not enough to overcome an enemy. One *must* have a well-armed aircraft. If only the Ki-27s were to carry 20-mm. machine guns! Couldn't you ask the commander to have them fitted?'

Fujisaki pursed his lips. He looked at me as if I had gone off my head. My logical mind had pushed me into making a totally uncalled-for demand. He rejected my proposition categorically and with uncharacteristic severity. Perhaps he had interpreted my idea as an unwarranted complaint.

He stood up, then said to me: 'I understand how you feel. I too know that one cannot destroy our adversary with 7.7-mm. machine guns, but all the same I shall take command of the Ki-27 formation on the next sortie. It is a fighter pilot's duty to make war with the equipment given to him. He must *never* complain. Even with the most wretched and obsolete airplanes, one can demonstrate one's ability. It is our task to acquire total command of any plane whatsoever and exploit it to the full. And, above all, I recommend you to refrain from making complaints. Yes, the Ki-27 is outdated and poorly armed, but even a 7.7-mm. bullet can kill a pilot. Aim at him! I am not really a fatalist, but I believe it is all the same whether we do everything we can to shoot down an antagonist, or nothing at all. Fate and skill are the only things that count. A pilot must bear these two vital elements in mind.'

He took off his helmet, scratched his head, and finally gratified me with one of those typical smiles of his. He was watching to see my reaction. He waved one hand vaguely in the air. I could see quite well what he was getting at. I nodded and replied: 'I understand, sir!' His encouraging smile broadened into a grin.

'Good!' he said, putting on his helmet again. 'In a few days, we shall certainly see the Superfortresses again. Keep your courage up! I'm going off on my night flight.'

He saluted and walked swiftly out of the mess. He had been quite right to reprove me for my facile suggestion. Rearming the Ki-27s would take considerable time, and besides, the added weight of the heavier machine guns would drastically, and perhaps fatally, diminish manoeuvrability. There were not enough Ki-45 Kais to confront the enemy bombers, so the Ki-27s had to be used and our only recourse was to make the best possible use of the available means. This conclusion cleared my mind of all troublesome ideas and, instead of being disappointed, I felt relieved by Fujisaki's admonition.

Only ten days remained of what had been one of the most eventful and disturbing years of my life, 1944. One morning, I woke up before reveille had sounded, which was unusual, as I was generally so exhausted that I slept like a dormouse. It was still dark. I looked at the luminous dial of my watch: 0540. For one instant, in the profound silence and solitude of the night, I imagined ice-candies whirling through the darkness. An extraordinary sensation! Restless and excited, I had a presentiment that something was going to happen. Not usually given to believing in premonitions, I felt this curious agitation that invaded me so strongly, although I could in no way explain it, that I was convinced a B-29 air raid would take place that day.

At 0600 hours, sharp and clear, the bugle shattered the silence. After parade, I clambered hastily into my flying suit and ran to the airstrip. The dawn was still tentative; the sky

over the sea retained its milky blue. An icy winter wind
brought the blood to my cheeks. The rising sun began to
tinge the peaks of the mountains with crimson. The weather
promised fine. Suddenly, my premonition transformed itself
into absolute certainty: the Superfortresses would carry out a
raid. Since the beginning of December, they had taken advantage of clear skies to improve their bombing precision and
score the maximum number of direct hits. They had a first-class
bomb-aimer, the Norden, but flying above the clouds made
precision impossible. Their incendiary bombs were not always
successful in setting fire to our houses, built of wood and paper.
I looked steadily towards the west, the direction from which
they would invade northern Kyushu.

At about 0800 hours, we were taking breakfast in the mess: a
bowl of rice, some *misoshiru* [Japanese soup], and some dried
fish. Suddenly, we heard a loudspeaker shrilling: three inter-
mittent rings. Preliminary warning! We were all ears. 'Attention!' announced the loudspeaker. '*Aka* forty, *yama* fifty! All
pilots report immediately to the briefing room!' *Aka*, Japanese
for 'red', was the code word for 'enemy'. *Aka* forty meant forty
aircraft. *Yama*, Japanese for 'mountain', signified the altitude,
in this case 16,250 feet, expressed in aviators' language. We all
leapt to our feet and rushed to the exit. Fujisaki stopped me in
the passage. 'Now,' he exclaimed, 'you're about to experience
your first fight! You're not scared, are you? Listen, drink a
small cup of green tea. Drink it down like *saké*, it will calm
you.' He held out the green tea and I swallowed it at one gulp.
He winked at me, the familiar smile on his face.

In the briefing room, pilots were awaiting the commander.
Ground crews were already checking the engines. The roar of
the motors was deafening in the cold morning air. Several
mechanics, in charge of testing weapons, were firing machine
guns out to sea. I was used to hearing these sounds before a
sortie, but today I heard them differently. Although I was
confident that I would not lose my head, I felt strangely keyed
up. This tension of one's whole will was necessary in order to
confront the enemy. But I had never felt anything quite like it
before. Something was tying my heart in knots, and my entrails
seemed to be heaving. At the same time, a heavy weight
oppressed my chest, like angina, so that I could barely stand
still. It reminded me of the tension I had felt before taking the
extremely difficult high school examinations, only this time it

95

was infinitely more violent! Fear, emotion, impatience? Impossible to define it. I breathed deeply to steady myself, then deliberately gazed out over the sea. On that vast mirror of water, the sun reflected dazzlingly.

The commander soon arrived. He glanced at his watch and then, with the aid of the blackboard, gave us some explanations. The four flight leaders had already written up the composition of their formations. We hung on Takahashi's every word.

'Listen to me,' he said gravely, 'listen very carefully. Here are my orders. Attacking position: the Second Flight at thirteen thousand feet to the southwest of Yahata; First Flight at nine thousand seven hundred and fifty feet; Fourth Flight at sixty-five hundred feet; Third at thirty-two hundred and fifty feet. Altitude: Second Flight at twenty-two thousand and seven hundred and fifty feet; First at nineteen thousand five hundred feet; Fourth at sixteen thousand two hundred and fifty feet; Third at seventeen thousand feet. Radio silence except for the four flight leaders. Make your own way home. The First and Second Flights are above all responsible for keeping the enemy from invading the skies of this defensive zone. That is all.'

The 4th Flight was composed of fifteen Ki-27s, piloted by seven cadet pilots, including myself, and an equal number of N.C.O.'s who had many more flying hours to their credit. Normally, only pilots with over 1,000 flying hours were qualified to engage the enemy in battle, but, since the beginning of 1944, we had suffered such heavy losses amongst pilots that even those who had only 500 to 600 hours received orders to go out on sortie. Circumstances no longer permitted us to wait till pilots were fully trained. Naval Air Fleet pilots were in the same position.

Flying Officer Fujisaki, leading the 4th Flight, gathered his fourteen pilots around him.

'Our mission,' he said, 'is to assault the enemy bombers who slip past the First and Second Flights. Each attack will be carried out in formations of two. The N.C.O.'s will endeavour to protect the trainees who are not sufficiently experienced. We have only Ki-27s in our flight. During combat, use the remarkable agility of this plane to the limit! If we cannot bring down the enemy craft, the Third Flight will take them on. Carry on, in short, just as you did during training . . .'

A ringing over the loudspeaker interrupted him. A single bell. It was the signal to scramble. 'All aircraft to take off!' shouted the commander eagerly. Each man ran to his plane. The maintenance crews started the motors. Dark-brown silhouettes, in fur-trimmed flying suits, spread out along the runway. I bounded into the seat of my Ki-27. A white circle painted round the fuselage just in front of the tail indicated that my plane was in service in the front line. I looked at it proudly. 'Everything O.K.!' said the mechanic. 'Good luck! I hope you shoot down a lot of B-29s!' I tried to smile at him . . . had I lost my serenity already? Without answering, I looked down the airstrip. Order of take-off: 2nd Flight first, 1st, 3rd and 4th to follow. Exactly twelve minutes after the scramble bell, I saw Flight Lieutenant Sanaka's Ki-45 Kai take off, leading the 2nd Flight. The Ki-45 Kais took off in succession. A few moments later, the 2nd Flight, in formation over the base, turned towards the west.

After the 3rd Flight, it was our turn. I was in the seventh plane in the formation. The patrol leader's plane took off, then zoomed skyward – a superb take-off! I nosed out on to the runway and lifted my plane into the air in the wake of the sixth aircraft. When taking off for attack, we did not wait for individual take-off signals. I gained altitude rapidly and rejoined the flight leader, who was circling over the mountain at 3,000 feet, waiting for us. Flight Sergeant Tanizaki, in the eighth plane, followed right on my tail. When the formation had joined up, our flight turned towards the west and gained altitude. I kept my eyes glued to the plane in front; this was no time to admire the clearness of the sky! The thought that I was actually going into action made me feel slightly feverish. Everything had undergone a transformation: the sky, as well as the very air I breathed. I was moving through an unknown world. It was not only a matter of fighting the enemy, but also of combating my own tendency to give way to panic.

When we reached our defensive position, I saw several placid-looking B-29s in the distance. In the wintry sun, their wings shone like neon signs. They were not as high as I had expected: between 13,000 and 14,500 feet. Long white trails streamed behind them, as if they had underestimated the fire-power of our little fighters and been hit. Fluttering around them were black dots, our Ki-45 Kais. They looked like pebbles bouncing off the huge walls of those gigantic fortresses built in the sky. The enemy bombers approached us, one behind the other.

Abruptly, Fujisaki waggled his wings – the signal to deploy into fighting formation! At 16,000 feet, there was some cloud. Followed by Tanizaki, I dropped down and dived into the cloud to conceal myself. A very odd thing: I was no longer terrified. The closer I got to the enemy, the less I feared death. I thought of nothing but shooting them down.

Emerging from the cloud, I discovered a B-29 about 1,300 feet below me, flying northeast. I dived. At 900 feet, two upper turrets on the Fortress opened fire. Tanizaki dived towards the bomber's tail, trying to wipe out the rear gun and so facilitate my attack. As I had foreseen, the rear upper turret began launching 12.7-mm. ice-candies at Tanizaki's plane. I took advantage of this to make a determined approach; at 650 feet, I discharged a burst of fire from both my 7.7-mm. machine guns by way of setting the aim correctly, then launched my ice-candies at the B-29s nose. I was aiming at the pilot. Magnificent fireworks! But my cockpit was riddled with bullet holes; to evade the bomber's fire, I had to go into a rapid side-slip, and this blurred my aim. My bullets spent themselves in the void. Just as I was about to get clear with a tight zoom climb, I caught a glimpse of two motionless figures in the cockpit of the bomber; they looked like dummies, and their calm air incited me to fury. Tanizaki, before rejoining me, let off his ice-candies at the nose of the enemy plane. By the time we regained our attacking altitude, the B-29 was already too far away. I must confess I was astounded at the speed of the Superfortress. Our Ki-27s were like gadflies on the back of a large, impassive cow. One flick of her tail, and the gadflies scattered.

Accompanied by Flight Sergeant Tanizaki, I attacked two other bombers flying in the wake of the first. Totally immersed in the action, I was indifferent to life, death, fear. My mind was concentrated solely on the attacking manoeuvres. This was reality. The Ki-27 was very easy to handle and it was not necessary to keep one's eyes incessantly on the instrument panel. Moreover, we had ordinary aircraft fuel instead of that foul A-Go. In these conditions, flying was simple. Sight the enemy, aim and fire, that was all I had to do. But each time I had to side-slip to escape the enemy's fire, the movement of the plane, and its position, made my aim very unreliable. I was forced to admit that there was a great difference between training and actual fighting. Alas! I was not capable of bringing down an adversary.

Having exhausted my ammunition, I showed the back of my hand to Tanizaki, to indicate that I was returning to base. He shook his head. Perhaps he still had some ammunition and intended to stalk other B-29s, on their way back from bombing Yahata and Kokura. I climbed to gain altitude. I circled above him at 16,250 feet. A few moments later, I saw a B-29 flying towards the west; it looked strange, and I thought it must have been damaged by our Ki-45 Kais. Tanizaki attacked. His ice-candies thudded into the wings and fuselage. I expected to see the B-29 fall down in flames, yet nothing happened. Our 7.7-mm. bullets were impotent to hurt this monster! Devoured by impatience and a most uncharacteristic impulse to violence, I would have liked to ram my plane into the mammoth Super-fortress. Its invulnerability goaded me to fury. Swiftly, Tanizaki rocket-climbed to join me: he too had used up his ammunition. With its nose pointed up, his Ki-27 seemed to have lost its usual brisk and nimble air, and to be crying tears of pity, rage and frustration.

Dispirited, Tanizaki and I landed. After reporting to the commander, I went to bed without even taking off my flying suit. I was worn out. Sleep overwhelmed me. I needed to sleep, if only for a few minutes, before making another sortie to take on the second wave of enemy planes.

That evening, I wrote in my diary: 'First air battle. Result: nil. I realise now how difficult it is to fire accurately in the air. Our lack of training is indisputably against us. It is almost impossible to shoot down the Superforts with 7.7-mm. bullets, but it would be cowardly to complain. The 4th Flight, all Ki-27s, met with no success, but the other three flights, composed of Ki-45 Kais, brought down a total of nine B-29s. I cannot clearly remember my own manoeuvres: all I can see is the bright fire of the ice-candies and the arrogant silhouettes of the enemy pilots. For a moment, driven by rage, I wanted to beat the enemy, even at the cost of my own life. I was mistaken in thinking a pilot must be logical and remain a human being during combat. Mere nonsense! Obviously, a pilot must keep a cool head at all times, but can there be one single pilot who always acts reasonably, and bears in mind the irreplaceable nature of a human life? If such a man exists, he must be a madman. Fighting in the air demands absolute contempt for death. Happy is he who has time to indulge in long-winded lucubrations! Surprisingly, at this moment, I no longer see that famous black speck which, for me, symbolised death and was a constant threat to me. It has completely disappeared. I have searched for it conscientiously, but it is no longer in front of my eyes. Have I, then, lost my obsession with death? Have I become indifferent to life itself? My first battle in the air has thrown all my convictions, feelings, sensations, into utter confusion. During combat, I did not even notice the swelling in my right leg. . . . '

The cadet pilots celebrated the New Year in the mechanics' quarters. The evening before, Squadron Leader Takahashi had said to us: 'As cadet pilots, you instantly received the rank of warrant officers, but you have no experience of military life and you have never been in contact with ordinary serving men. . . . Now, it is indispensable for an officer to know the mentality of his soldiers. Your conduct has a strong influence upon their morale. In a sense, it is more difficult to command a troop under fire than it is to fight an air battle. A superior must always share the pains and the joys of his subordinates. From tomorrow, you will spend five days in the mechanics' quarters so as to get to know them better.'

Our first surprise was the difference in the food. The ground crews were really undernourished. Even though it was New Year, they had to make do with really scrappy meals: a bowl of maize with a little rice and a few vegetables – not a morsel of meat. And not a drop of *saké* to celebrate the arrival of 1945! Where, then, did they get their energy that kept them working forty-eight hours non-stop on the job of repairing planes? Was it sheer willpower? They all looked sickly, yet not one of them ever complained of his lot. How I pitied them! Their devotion inspired our respect. The food crisis was indeed severe if soldiers at a fighting base had to put up with such miserable food. It shocked me. Could Japan still be hoping to pull of a final victory? It was impossible to feel anything but pessimistic. New Year was the most important festival, normally celebrated by our people with great display and generous quantities of *saké*. Alas! There was nothing like this to usher in 1945. I felt a deep melancholy.

Our losses in pilots and planes were becoming heavier all the time. I no longer expected to live till the end of the year; this would be the last New Year of my life. My heart shrank at the horrible premonition that, when 1946 came in, I would no longer be in this world. I was alive only out of habit. Yet I was burning with the desire to shoot down the gigantic Superfortresses, and this very desire gave a wartime pilot a reason for living and fighting to the bitter end. It was more important to score victories than to cling cautiously to life. War was undeniably monstrous and inhuman, but from the moment one became a cell – albeit a minute one – in this juggernaut called war, there was no point condemning it and preaching humanism. If there were regrets in my heart, they were not due to philosophical nostalgia, but to shame that I had not shot down an enemy bomber. Of course, we were short on training and experience! And our little Ki-27s were powerless before the stupefying fire-power of the large bombers. Their central firing computer, controlling the gun turrets by remote control, had proved extraordinarily efficient. An isolated B-29, on a photographic mission one day over the Nipponese archipelago, had been attacked by more than ninety of our fighters, and, lo and behold, the enemy plane, which was not equipped for a bombing mission, managed to repulse their attack by climbing to a very high altitude and putting on all possible speed. During this battle, which lasted more than half an hour, he shot down seven of our fighters and finally escaped.

Japan had a reserve of about 1,000 planes. It was evident that our army would soon be without an effective air fleet. Most of our pilots were inexperienced; courage and relentlessness had to make up for lack of skill. Personally, as a pilot, I had shown myself to be unequal to the task in hand, and I felt a certain shame before the ground crews.

The 1st of January passed like any other day. No doubt in the pilots' billets, they were celebrating it with *saké* . . . but here, in the evening, thirty N.C.O.'s and soldiers of the 3rd Squadron of maintenance crews lined up for roll call in their quarters. Beneath the dim light of the shaded bulbs, their faces looked glum. Harassed by overwork, they had only one desire: to sleep. But there were chores to be done even after roll call: boots to polish, officers' linen to wash and so on.

Ten minutes before the duty officer came round to inspect

the sleeping quarters, a leading aircraftman and a veteran soldier made a sudden spot check to make sure the men had put the safety catches on their rifles, which were ranged along a rack. Sometimes, soldiers did, in fact, forget to do this after cleaning them, and, since leaving a weapon loaded for several hours was liable to have a deleterious effect on the sights, they were supposed to unload them as well. Uneasily, the soldiers followed the two veterans; each man heaved an audible sigh of relief when his own rifle passed inspection. Clack! a sharp sound broke the silence. Someone had committed the sin of omitting to unload his rifle. The N.C.O. looked sternly at the men and then yelled: 'Whose is this?'

'Mine, Leading Aircraftman,' replied a soldier, standing to attention.

It was Munakata, an aircraftman Second Class. He was a man of forty and a teacher of mineralogy at a college of higher education in a town in Kyushu. The manpower crisis had forced the army to recruit men of forty and over, even those who were in indifferent health.

'I beg your pardon, Leading Aircraftman,' said Munakata, his face ashen.

'Do you think apologising is enough?' bellowed the N.C.O.

I could read in Munakata's eyes the terror and anguish that was clutching at his heart. What exemplary punishment would be meted out to this second-class airman? He might not get away with a routine disciplinary action. The mechanics looked at the N.C.O. holding their breath. Just at that moment, the duty officer came into the billet. Relief showed on their faces. Nevertheless, as soon as the officer went out, after taking roll call, the N.C.O. summoned A.C.2 Munakata. The young recruits made a show of polishing their seniors' shoes, not daring to look up for fear of getting drawn into the affair.

'Right, now, the bicycle!' cried the N.C.O. to Munakata. 'Keep pedalling till I authorise you to stop!'

This was an idiotic punishment: the victim was made to stand in the gap between two tables, rest his hands on either side of him, then lift his body up by pressing down on his hands and imitate the pedalling movements of a cyclist. The old soldiers formed a circle round Munakata. His face was blood-red with shame and indignation. To this suppressed rage was added physical suffering, for each turn of the imaginary pedal was as hard as climbing a steep stair.

'Now then, you're going uphill,' said one of the N.C.O.'s.

He smiled, but there was a hint of ferocity on his lips. Munakata made his legs move in space like a watermill. Pain and humiliation contorted his features.

'You see an officer on your left,' shouted a veteran for a joke.

The poor soldier put one foot on the floor so as to raise his right hand and salute the imaginary officer. All the veterans burst out laughing, then fell to thumping him with their fists. 'Who gave you permission to put your foot on the ground?' they barked at him, 'Keep pedalling!'

What lunacy! I recalled vividly what Yao, my ex-comrade from Shizuoka High School had related to me. He had not been exaggerating. The N.C.O.'s were always devising new punishments, they positively gloated over the preparation of their sadistic sessions. What motivated this brutality? At Naval Academy, officer cadets were not permitted to hold private conversations with N.C.O.'s, and they were constantly indoctrinated with the idea that their inferiors in rank should be treated like animals. The N.C.O.'s knew this, and this unjust prejudice against them stirred up their bile and led them to take their revenge. Tormented and despised themselves, they took delight in tormenting others. It was all grossly unfair. They had no reason to hate the recruits, and it would have been better if they had vented their spleen on the enemy, not their own compatriots.

It was a completely different matter with N.C.O. pilots. They showed no jealousy towards the cadet pilots, who were their seniors in rank, notwithstanding their lack of military experience. For example, Flight Sergeant Tanizaki, a very disciplined and obedient airman, had made every effort to protect me during the fight in the air, without seeking to carry off a personal success. It is true that actual combat engenders this innate solidarity that binds all pilots into one fraternity, which also includes the ground crews. They understand and love one another.

This hate-inspired punishment, then, was the vengeance of the weak. Far from inspiring a soldier to reflect on his culpable negligence and mend his ways, it led to an aversion to military life. The veterans were, moreover, much younger and less educated than Munakata. They might have been his sons, or his pupils. The man must have been deeply wounded in his self-respect, and with every justification, for the punishment was far too gross for the offence and could only succeed in reinforcing a spirit of insubordination. I was writing, pretending not to notice this ludicrous scene. Munakata, following the orders of the veterans, again began pedalling like an acrobat. Suddenly, I sprang to my feet and shouted: 'Stop!' I walked towards the leading aircraftman. In the silence that ensued, I looked at his broad shoulders; somehow, they expressed bitterness. Fuming, we stood face to face.

'Leading Aircraftman,' I said to him, 'it is strictly forbidden to torture the men! You are well aware of this. This evening, I will close my eyes to your offence against military discipline, but do not make such a mistake again. You go too far. Remember, there is a limit to all things. Haven't you seen the white circles painted on the planes you service every day? Those are the marks of planes in the front line, for Japan herself is already a battlefield. Nothing is more absurd than to waste energy fighting amongst ourselves instead of fighting the enemy. Your sadistic torments are not likely to inspire good discipline. You must learn to handle the men wisely.'

The N.C.O. shrugged, as if it was a matter of no importance. He looked at me with hostility, as if to say: 'In the army, it's experience that counts, not rank. You're just a greenhorn. Keep your nose out of it!' In spite of myself, I was so incensed that I struck him several times. Then I ordered everyone to go to bed and get some sleep, as there might be an enemy raid at dawn.

The men scrambled to finish their tasks, and then slithered down into their beds. Without taking my eyes off him, I awaited the leading aircraftman's reaction. His face was so expressive that I was vividly aware of what was passing in his mind. Finally, he lowered his eyes and said dejectedly: 'I understand, Cadet Pilot! I am sorry. I apologise . . . '

'Munakata is an intelligent and well-educated man,' I said to him by way of conclusion. 'He will respond much better to a stern reprimand than to violence and mockery. Well, now, good night!'

The bugle sounded lights-out. I slipped down into my bed. Almost at once, I heard footsteps approaching. Someone was standing near me, saying in a quavering voice: 'I cannot thank you enough, Cadet Pilot.' It was Munakata. His regular, oval face and the tortoise-shell frames of his glasses had reminded me of Professor Arinaga, my old French teacher. He was a typical-looking academic. I would have liked to use the formal address to him, as a mark of respect, but the disparity of our rank forbade it. Discipline first and foremost! Especially as I had just been preaching to the N.C.O. the necessity of not infringing it! The veterans were probably listening, not wanting to miss a word of our conversation. If I had shown the slightest intimacy or kindness towards Munakata, he would have suffered reprisals, so I merely whispered to him, with affected coldness: 'Take better care of your rifle in future!'

I could not sleep; the unpleasant scene I had just witnessed kept running through my head, and my own violent reaction to the N.C.O. disgusted me: I had never before struck an inferior. Some of the cadet pilots treated other ranks with brutality, saying in self-justification: 'Corporal punishment is necessary in certain cases. The lower ranks are crafty by nature and full of tricks. They are shirkers too. Only physical suffering wakes them up and makes them realise they belong to the Imperial Army.' A dubious piece of reasoning. It was rather that the men were whipping boys, on whom the officers let out the frustrations of their own harsh life. Although they were not actually struck, the very junior officers had to undergo severe trials.

One of the many things that tried their nerves was waiting for air raids. During those hours, their gall accumulated and worked in them like an illness. So then they would vent their spleen on the men beneath them, using the need for discipline as an ever-handy pretext. But it was inexcusable weakness, or so it seemed to me, for what they should have done was go to their leaders and rage against the absurdity of army life.

Nevertheless, this evening, in spite of my convictions, I had hit a leading aircraftman in the face. I had ridiculed him in front of his men, and this would only make him more brutal with them: a vicious circle. In Japan, as elsewhere, we make good resolutions at New Year. My father often said: 'Be careful! If you swallow medicine on New Year's Day, you will have to take it many times throughout the year.' I had never taken him seriously. Now, I vowed that I would keep an absolute control over myself, even during battle. Moreover, I would never again succumb to violence and never ill-treat my men.

The five days I spent in the ground crews' billets impressed me only with the wretchedness of their existence. Ludicrous punishments, miserable food, hypocrisy – all this could eventually undermine morale. But it was not the business of a lowly cadet pilot to remedy matters.

Idleness is the mother of all vices: daily life, without flying and without action, had plunged my mind into upsetting channels of thought, and I took a gloomy view of the outcome of the war. I realised that, for a pilot, action in the air becomes a sort of basic need.

My future had shrunk to a finite perspective; every second was irretrievable. I must live intensely, so that I could die without regrets. Happily, training on the Ki-45 Kais began on the 6th of January. Gone at once were my nostalgia, meditations on the stupidity of the army and pondering on death!

Changing over from the lightweight Ki-27 to the Ki-45 Kai was like exchanging a racehorse for a carthorse. The problems of flying this aircraft, which was entirely new to me, arose from its weight and from the fact that it was twin-engined, unlike the Ki-27.

It was difficult to get it airborne; I dared not wrench it forcibly off the ground in case it stalled. Sometimes it ran along the runway for a distance of more than 3,000 yards, hopping and bouncing on its undercarriage like a dragonfly skimming over the surface of the water. Flight Lieutenant Sanaka's dazzling take-off inspired my envy; he was able to lift off after only the briefest run and handled his Ki-45 as easily as if it had been a motor scooter.

This heavy fighter could execute almost all the aerobatic manoeuvres: looping-the-loop, Immelmann, inverted flying. But one had to keep one's eyes glued to the instrument panel, because it was very dangerous to rely on guesswork when indulging in aerobatics. For example, when doing a zoom climb, a mishandling of the throttle would inevitably cause a stall at the moment of levelling out to a horizontal position. As for looping-the-loop, one had to keep an eye on the engine r.p.m. indicator, especially when flying in the inverted position. However, in this position, the pilot's trunk left the seat so that his head touched the roof of the cockpit, making it difficult to read the r.p.m. indicator. I had been longing to leave that wretched, obsolete Ki-27 behind me and fly the Ki-45 Kai, but I had never expected to find the plane so difficult to handle! But the army had no other machine capable of shooting down the giant American bombers, so I had to apply myself to the best of my ability.

At that period, we had few heavy fighters of this type, so they were very precious and we handled them with the greatest circumspection.

It was a terribly hard winter. All the pilots, including Flight Lieutenants Sanaka and Togashi, participated in the frequent fatigue of clearing snow from the airstrip. It was essential work, but the enemy did not always allow us time to do it! One day when I was on snow-clearing fatigue, a soldier came running from the guard room to tell me I had a visitor. It could not be my father. Who was it? A young man in the black uniform of a university student was waiting for me: it was Nozawa. He had been a member of our baseball team at Shizuoka High School. He was currently studying physics at the Imperial University of Kyushu (at Fukuoka). The Minister of State Education had banned baseball, and our club was dissolved in 1944; since then, Nozawa and I had seen each other only at long intervals.

I was very grateful to him for taking the trouble to visit me at Ozuki. We tapped each other on the shoulder. He stared at me before speaking. I was wearing my flying suit.

'Well, well!' he said. 'I wouldn't have recognised you . . . the perfect airman! I thought I'd look in on you on my way back to Fukuoka. I've been to Tokyo to see my parents, and I visited your family in the country. Your mother asked me to give you this parcel. . . . '

'How kind of you!' I said, taking the little package.

I bombarded him with questions. Were all the family well? What was my mother doing? Was she going for walks every day? She loved arranging flowers, and I could imagine her bending over the blossoms and choosing the ones she would pick. Now that this wonderful winter had gripped the countryside, was she happily occupied indoors, busy with her housework?

'Have you heard anything of Suzuki, Oshima and Saga? Are you enjoying life at the Imperial University?' Nozawa had received no news of my three close friends since they left high school.

I went into the reception room with him. A pilot and a rather elderly woman were sitting in a corner; she was undoubtedly his mother. He was combing her long, beautiful hair with a little wooden comb. I know of no more touching sight: it is a proof of a great tenderness between mother and son. Perhaps this was his last act of filial piety. The moment they saw us, they stood up. It was Flight Sergeant Tanizaki and his mother. The lady, who was simply dressed, bowed low, while Tanizaki saluted me, then said: 'Cadet Pilot, allow me to introduce my mother to you.' She looked at me timidly.

'Officer,' she said, 'I wish to thank you sincerely for all you have done for my boy. He is the eldest of my three sons. He always wanted to be a pilot and aviators were his heroes. He is very happy to be flying fighters. . . . Is he a good pilot?'

I assured her that her son was an excellent pilot. Afraid my presence would embarrass the flight sergeant and his mother, I invited Nozawa to come to the trainees' sitting room with me, but he had no time. He had a train to catch and the station was some distance away. I walked to the gate with him. He asked me for a cigarette and I gave him two packets. He lit one avidly at once, for, he told me between puffs, he had not smoked for a week. I was sorry for him. As I knew he was a heavy smoker. I would have willingly have given him all the cigarettes I had. What joy it had been to see a friend again! I watched him disappear into the distance, the cigarette dangling from his lips.

Back in our quarters, I opened the parcel Nozawa had brought me. It contained both volumes of George Sand's *Les Maîtres Sonneurs*! My mother knew how I loved this novel. This was indeed a gesture of motherly love! I held them in my hand for a few moments, thinking of my mother, and I felt like kissing them. I wanted to re-read this pastoral romance before I died, yet I had not admitted this desire to anyone. Amongst the first pages, I rediscovered my pencilled margin notes. I had written in the translation of words I was unfamiliar with. I cannot express the emotion I felt when I looked at the title, and at these notes. Would I have time to read this beloved book again? I stowed the two volumes carefully in my drawer, then returned to the airfield.

It was the end of January. According to information gathered by reconnaissance planes, the Americans were about to carry out a daylight raid on northern Kyushu. The enemy formation consisted of almost seventy Superfortresses. A single shrill ring sent all the Ki-45 Kais of the 4th Squadron racing into the air. The thirty-six planes divided up into three flights. I belonged to the third, commanded by Flight Lieutenant Togashi. The higher I climbed into the air, the faster my heart beat; I felt my blood boil at the thought of the imminent fight. I had made a stoic, absolute resolution: to bring down an adversary at all costs. There was no place in my mind for fear of death or love of life. If someone had said to me at that moment: 'You are not a professional soldier, but a cultivated man, and a pacifist; you would do better to spend your time in philosophical meditation rather than allowing yourself to be carried away by frenzy!' I would have despised him utterly.

In the sky southwest of Kokura, the 3rd Flight caught sight of the enemy. *Yama* 50 (altitude 15,000 feet), favourable for precision bombing. Togashi, followed by two other planes, waggled his wings as a signal for the formation to spread out, and launched the first attack. In tenth position, I continued flying westward in the hope of intercepting another enemy aircraft. A few minutes later, I discovered a B-29 flying towards the industrial city. It had that cheeky 'catch-me-if-you-can' air about it. I looked back at the eleventh Ki-45 Kai, piloted by Tanizaki, which was immediately behind me. He raised his hand in response and smiled at me, his face full of courage.

I charged at the B-29 from below and to starboard, letting go my 12.7-mm. tracer bullets. They passed under the wing: my aim was short! Ice-candies fired from the gun turret in the waist of the Superfortress grazed my fuselage. In that instant, I changed direction suddenly, to take aim at the right side. Tanizaki's plane slipped under the belly of the American plane, firing 20-mm. bullets. I took advantage of this to lift the nose of my craft and press the button on my 20-mm. machine guns. But my bullets sputtered into the void. Just at the moment when I was about to break away with a wing-over, I distinctly saw the ruddy cheeks of the enemy pilot. After the wing-over, I dived steeply to return to the attack. My plane was quivering like a leaf. I glanced at the air speed indicator: nearly 300 miles per hour. This was the maximum permitted speed and it

109

was dangerous to exceed it. It felt as if the wings were about to crumple. I would have liked to dive again, so as to regain my attacking position with all possible speed, but it would have meant running the risk of tearing the ailerons off. They were, in fact, the weak point of the Ki-45 Kai. I contented myself with levelling out. The Superfortress was now heading northwest; one of the two starboard engines was spitting black smoke. It was returning to base: Tanizaki's 20-mm. bullets had hit it.

Tanizaki's plane should have been behind mine. I looked round. Nothing. Where was it? I finally spotted it way below me at 5 o'clock. It was bucketing about like a drunken man. I decided to leave the B-29 to its fate and dived down to rejoin Tanizaki's plane, which was visibly losing altitude. As I drew level with him, I could see his head lolling back against the seat. His helmet and silk scarf were stained with blood: the B-29s bullets had found their mark. I overtook him with the aim of guiding him to the nearest airstrip. But he was too gravely wounded, he could do no more. He looked at me for a moment with eyes that were already dim and, with a great effort, saluted me as a gesture of farewell. I tried desperately to rouse him by some encouraging sign, but he gently replied 'no' with his head; he was at the very end of his strength. I shouted like a maniac: 'Courage, Tanizaki! Courage!' although I knew he could not hear me. A few seconds later, I saw his head drop forward suddenly and the plane plunged into a nose dive. I saluted his plane, which had gone into a tail spin and was rapidly dwindling out of sight. 'Thank you, Tanizaki!' I murmured. 'You saved my life. I shall avenge you.'

I gained altitude to close with an enemy. Over Kokura, two Ki-45 Kais were repeatedly attacking a B-29, and I was foolhardy enough to create a diversion by flying over the American plane. My heart was thirsting for revenge, but all my bullets missed their mark. After a minute or so, the two other Ki-45 Kais, having exhausted their ammunition, turned back to base. Mine too was exhausted; owing to the shortage of supplies, we were not always able to fill the magazines of our machine guns. Crying with frustration, I changed course and made for the airfield. The Superfortress had slipped safely away.

Once more, I returned with negative results. I was a complete failure. I cannot express the shame I felt. As soon as the all-clear sounded, I hurried to the N.C.O.'s billets; I crossed the room and stopped, facing Tanizaki's bed. Some sticks of incense had already been lit in front of the possessions he had left behind. His immaculate cap seemed to say to me: 'This man sacrificed his life to defend you.' He had signed on for fifteen years as a *shonen-hikohei*, but now, after only five years, he had been despatched to the other world. His was a heroic death. In my mind's eye, I saw again Tanizaki combing his mother's hair, saluting me for the last time, then hurtling down. This image became a nightmare and the nightmare pierced my soul. I picked up the piece of paper that had been placed on his cap: it was a letter addressed to his mother. He had not had time to finish it. I read: 'My dear Mother, my soul will always have its home on the moon, even after my death. If you feel sad, look at the moon, in all its beauty. You will find me again up there. . . . ' Tears sprang to my eyes. It seemed to me the N.C.O.'s were looking at me coldly. I bowed before the empty bed and left the room without saying a word to his comrades.

At the end of January, the 20th U.S. Bomber Command, based in China, was transferred to the Marianas. The Americans formed the 20th Air Force there, with a strength that included more than 100 B-29s. By March, they would have 300. The purpose of the transfer was to permit the Superfortresses to carry the maximum number of bombs when raiding the large cities on the Nipponese archipelago. The U.S. Combined General Staff believed that the only means by which they could force us to capitulate was by landing their troops on our soil. To achieve this, they were ready to pulverise everything. Once they had gained mastery of the sea, there was nothing to prevent the Task Force fighters from accompanying the formations of bombers. And so, henceforth, we would be up against not only the Superfortresses, but also the finest fighter planes in existence.

In mid-February, twenty-six trainees from the 4th Squadron were transferred to the 24th Squadron for advanced training. We were to learn how to combat the American fighters. To my great regret, I left the 4th Squadron without having shot down a B-29. But I had to obey orders.

Lieutenant Fujisaki a last visit. He invited me to sit down,

Two hours before leaving the base, I went to pay Flight

smiling as always, then said: 'You're leaving, we shall never see each other again. The navy has already invented suicide-attacks, and sooner or later we fighter pilots will have to resort to the same tactics. Do you believe in a life beyond the grave?'

Rather embarrassed, I mumbled: 'No, sir, I am more or less an atheist.'

He drank the rest of his green tea and looked fixedly into the bottom of the cup. I filled it up.

'Me too,' he sighed. 'The Buddhists still believe in life after death, but it is absurd. When I was a student at university, I often went to the Buddhist temples, even though I am not of that religion. And I did not go in to pray, but to admire the statues of Buddha. I loved their soft lines, and found them very interesting. You know, although this sculpture is flat, almost two-dimensional, it has a mysterious beauty, a serenity, which I do not find in Greek sculpture. The latter have very pronounced features, especially if you imagine how they must look in the strong sunlight of Greece. All the same, there is too much gloom in Buddhism, and in their temples, don't you agree?'

'Yes, I do,' I said. 'The bonze [priest] always preaches about hell rather than heaven. Besides, the legend of the river that flows past the gates of hell and has to be crossed by dead souls repels me. I cannot see myself, wrapped in a shroud, paying the ferryman my fare, while the icy wind howls around us. . . . When I was a child, a bonze said to me: 'Never tell lies, little one, or you will suffer the torments of hell. . . . ' Well, one day I told my pals a little lie, and for several days after that, I was obsessed by the horrific spectacle he had described to me. It's inhuman. I have given up Buddhism once and for all.'

'Perhaps you are right. After death, there is nothing but oblivion. I cannot imagine myself reincarnated as a tree, a blade of grass, a rock. It's ridiculous! If it were true, how could one trample on the grass, or walk over rocks which, according to the Buddhists, are inhabited by the souls of our ancestors? Religion should seek to exalt life and not to inspire us with a terror of death. Basically, it's a drug. When all is said and done, death is the end of everything. Afterwards, there is nothingness. Even the soul disappears without a trace. Ah, well,' Fujisaki concluded cheerfully, 'we have enjoyed more than twenty years of happiness, and the affection of our

112

families. What more could one ask? Who cares what happens to me after my death! It is impossible, unthinkable, that we should see each other again in the hereafter, even through the intermediary of our souls. And now, I shall say goodbye to you, forever. . . . '

Part Three

'My dear parents,
I shall depart this life at 07.00 hours.' . . .

Forty miles north-northwest of Tokyo, there is a little village called Kagohara; a dirt road bordered with young elm trees and old single-storey houses runs through it from east to west. Very few vehicles pass that way, other than army lorries. Even in this remote neck of the woods, the total absence of petrol had an effect: carts loaded with wood raised clouds of dust that settled on the rooftops and caused the inhabitants to complain bitterly. From the little station, this road ran as far as a crossroads where there stood a stone statue of Buddha, sheltered beneath a minuscule shrine that had been much battered by wind and rain. There were always a few sticks of incense burning in front of the statue. Perhaps the women of the village were offering up prayers for their sons or husbands. As you turned north, taking the track between two fields, you came across a barracks, about half a mile farther on. This was where the 24th Advanced Training Squadron was stationed. The entrances were guarded night and day with extreme vigilance; you would have thought you were already at the battlefront.

Marching from Kagohara station in the late morning, the cadet pilots choked in the thick, whitish dust. The cold, sharp wind, which might be called the speciality of that region, swept up and whirled away the fallen leaves. The trainees raised their eyes in amazement to a sky in which there was not a single plane to be seen. Nevertheless, once through the barracks gate, they were happy to find the familiar and unique atmosphere of a miltary airfield: all the pilots who passed them, wearing flying suits, had that bright, piercing look of airmen. After reporting to Suenaga, the commanding officer of the squadron, they rushed to the airfield.

In one corner of the field stood a high metallic tower, with a steel cable stretched obliquely from the top of the tower to the ground. This was for landing training. The novice pilot learned to land by sitting in a kind of cable car and manipulating the control column. But the cable was covered in rust; evidently it was no longer used. At the beginning of the year, the Kumagaya Flying School had been closed and the 24th Advanced Training Squadron had taken over. There was a rumour that *tokusos* of the 4th Intake had been transferred to the Service Corps, due to the fuel crisis.

We went into one of the hangars. Nothing, except one Type 99 (Ki-55) trainer. We looked sorrowfully at one another. The maintenance crews stopped work and saluted us. One of our men accosted a mechanic and asked him rather irritably: 'Listen, doesn't this squadron possess any airplanes?'

'Yes, Cadet Pilot,' replied the N.C.O. hastily. 'The planes have just been taken into tunnels dug out in the woods round the aerodrome. We were afraid they'd be shot up by enemy machine guns.'

On February 16, American fighters based on aircraft carriers had, in fact, attacked the region of Kanto for the first time. This region includes Tokyo, Yokohama, Utsunomiya and Kagohara. Our air forces responsible for the defence of the Nipponese archipelago were extremely feeble: a total of 870 fighters. The 1st Army Air Fleet was composed solely of advanced training squadrons and the 6th had no more than about fifty planes. As for anti-aircraft guns, there were only 1,200. The destruction of even a single fighter was, therefore, a catastrophe, and we treasured our aircraft as if they were solid gold.

The differences of opinion between the Army General Staff and the government accentuated still further the gravity of the situation.

On December 19, 1944, the General Staff had broken off the Leyte operation without advising Prime Minister Koiso, who still believed that it was the central pivot of the war. It was the Emperor himself who informed Koiso. The astonished Prime Minister replied: 'Allow me to tell Your Imperial Majesty that it is extremely difficult for me to accomplish my task, when I am not even informed of the latest developments.' He was justifiably furious at being kept in the dark.

We ran to the edge of the woods. The cadet who was in front stopped abruptly and pointed to the runway, shouting:

118

'There they are!' And, indeed, we saw several planes camouflaged in dark green. From their shape, we were convinced they were Type 1 (Ki-43) fighters. As we approached them, however, we realised they were only mock-ups, clever models of the Ki-43. 'It's a trick to fool the Yankees!' said someone.

At last, we saw a real Ki-43 beneath a tunnel of branches. Planes were hidden in a number of these revetments. I looked at the elegant lines of this fighter, patently different from the Ki-27. It had a retractable undercarriage.

The Ki-43 was generally known as the *Hayabusa* (Falcon). First put into service in April, 1941, it was as agile as the Ki-27, but outclassed it in speed and range. Amongst the various models built, the three-propeller Ki-43 (the one I was now looking at) reached a speed of 320 miles per hour and had a range of about 1,000 miles. Armed with two 12.7-mm. machine guns and equipped with a 1,150-horsepower engine, it could reach a ceiling of 35,000 feet. The early models had developed 'teething troubles,' but they were famous all the same, especially at the beginning of the war, and the faults were later corrected. The 64th Squadron, under the command of Wing Commander Takeo Kato, although it possessed only forty planes, had been prodigiously active. Based in southern Indo-China, they had covered a very long range to reach Burma and Malaya. They had brought down a great many British fighters, to the astonishment of the British, who had not believed the Japanese had fighters capable of flying the more than 600 miles round trip between Singapore and their base. Neither the Buffaloes nor the Hellcats nor the P-40s were able to measure up to them. Even Japanese children sang 'The Song of the Falcon' in praise of Kato's Squadron and their feats of arms:

> With engines throbbing, full of power,
> Our Falcons fly above the clouds.
> A scarlet circle on each wing
> And on their breasts, an eagle . . .
> These are the marks of our squadron.

But when the P-38, P39 and P-51 made their appearance in the middle of 1943, our Ki-43s found themselves in difficulties, in spite of their excellent qualities. In the first place, they were too slow, and had to keep on the defensive, even against the P-47 and Grumman F-6-F, which were launched from aircraft carriers. Sometimes, however, they were loaded with bombs weighing from 60 to 200 pounds, in Guadalcanal or New Guinea, and attacked American shipping with these. But alas! Losses during these operations were far from negligible. Those that survived continued to take part in battle, for at least they were faster than the Ki-27s, which were also used against the B-29s.

That same evening, the cadet pilots mustered officially in the mess. Our C.O., Suenaga, looked into the eyes of each man before he spoke. He was obviously making an effort.

'We are extremely sorry to tell you,' he growled, 'that at this moment the squadron possesses not one drop of petrol. You will have noticed that there were no planes in the air today. So there will be no training for a few days, until the petrol arrives. In the meantime, Flight Lieutenant Uehara will teach you how to fight with the Ki-43. Between lectures, you will help your comrades in the ground crews to fabricate artificial planes. The duty officer will give you your duty roster daily. That is all.'

The task of building these imitation planes consisted in tying bamboos together in the form of an airplane and then covering them with leafy branches. They were dotted about here and there on the aerodrome, where they would not hamper the take-off and landing of planes. From close to, they were very gimcrack affairs, but they looked real enough from the air.

I had joined the air force to escape the boringly simple work of a factory, and also to serve my country more usefully. What an illusion! I had given up everything – my family, my studies, my home – to serve as a pilot, and now I was obliged to spend my time doing chores even a child could have done! Was I doomed to renounce my sole purpose? These puerile fatigues filled me with melancholy and made me a prey to morbid thoughts.

Flight Lieutenant Uehara's lessons redoubled our desire to fly. This officer was an ex-*shonen hikohei*, with fifteen years of military experience behind him. He had belonged to the 77th Squadron, which had fought so valiantly in New Guinea. Broad-shouldered and solidly-built, he always stood very straight when he spoke to us.

'By the way,' he said one day, holding in his hand two models of the Ki-43 and the Grumman F-6-F, 'the most important thing during an air battle is to be very daring. It is the only way you will find the courage to be your true selves. The

120

slightest hesitation may be fatal. . . . One day in 1943, our squadron ran into the Grumman F-6-F to the east of New Guinea . . . twenty of them against our nine Ki-43s. Flight Lieutenant Okaya, our flight leader, took advantage of our higher altitude to get right above the tail of the enemy flight leader's plane. He was a young regular officer with very high qualifications. I was piloting the second plane, whose task it is to prevent the leader from being shot down. I placed myself in a position to survey and protect Okaya's rear. At a hundred and thirty feet, he fired his twelve-seven-millimetre bullets. His aim was good and the enemy plane caught fire.'

Uehara stopped speaking for a moment, then looked up at the ceiling. He obviously cherished his memories.

'So then,' he went on, 'two Grummans zoomed up to face me. My biggest worry was the thirteen-millimetre machine guns fixed in the nose of the plane. There was a danger that my engine would be hit in a face-to-face confrontation. I climbed up, banking to the right and deliberately exposing my underbelly. I daresay they were thinking: 'What a bit of luck!' And, in fact, just then they unleashed a stream of bullets. On the spur of the moment, I changed course, dropping down and to the left, then fired as I flew down diagonally across them. Some of my bullets pierced the windshield and struck the pilot's body. His head lolled back, he looked as if he had been clubbed. I went into an Immelmann to the left before side-slipping across the front of the Grumman. My adversary went down in a tail spin. . . . At that instant, I was seized by a nameless terror. It is a horrifying moment when you bring down an enemy. You cannot help imagining yourself in the same situation!'

The flight lieutenant's voice rose excitedly. Everyone looked at him. It was as if each man was participating in a dogfight with an American fighter.

'Listen now!' he said, showing us the two models. 'I had seen a Grumman pursuing Flight Lieutenant Okaya. Unfortunately, as you know, the Ki-43 is slower than the F-6-F. I thought our leader would go into a vertical roll, which was his usual trick for giving the enemy the slip. But he went into a slow barrel roll! Look out! His adversary had a splendid chance to riddle Okaya's plane with bullets, for this manoeuvre had slowed him down. . . . Wham! The Grumman passed over him like a battering ram. This propitious moment was not lost on the flight lieutenant – he fired as he was flying in the inverted position. A stream of bullets darted out like a chameleon's tongue reaching for a morsel of food. They hit the target. Bravo! The bullets looked like cards being flicked through the air in perfect order by an expert dealer. That is the trick of fighting with the Ki-43 . . . if he had hesitated for an instant, he would have been shot down. What inspired him to risk the slow barrel roll? Nothing else but extraordinary daring! Now, do you understand?'

The actual reality of fighting in the air, as described to us by Uehara, excited our desire to pilot the Ki-43.

At the end of February, the squadron at last received supplies of petrol. For the first time, I piloted the pride of the army, the famous Falcon. What a difference the retractable undercarriage made! Moreover, the Ki-43 was just as manoeuvrable as the Ki-27. It could do all the aerobatic tricks. Doing the slow barrel roll, I thought of Flight Lieutenant Okaya's trick. Upside down, I pressed the machine gun trigger and riddled a fleecy cloud from top to bottom. Of course, the guns were not loaded, and I could not be sure of bringing off Okaya's stunning trick against a real adversary. But we had to get all the training we could; this was the only way we could acquire the daring exhorted of us by Flight Lieutenant Uehara. Fighting in the air demands precision, fine judgement, mental alertness. But alas! Due to the fuel shortage, we could train only one day in five.

Early in March, my parents came to see me. My two sisters had had to queue up all night to obtain the railway tickets. Civilian life was becoming almost unendurable, for even basic necessities were lacking.

'As a matter of interest,' I asked my father, 'have you still got those volumes of Marx's *Das Kapital* that you confiscated from me?'

During the summer of 1943, I had bought six volumes of the Japanese translation of *Das Kapital*. I had paid twenty yens for them – enough for one person to live on for a month; since censorship of public opinion had been enforced, this work was very difficult to obtain. I had taken the books home to Nagoya to read during the holidays. My father had been very upset at finding them on my desk, and had hidden them after saying to me: 'The secret police are watching high school and university students, as you know. They might even carry out a search without warning. You could be arrested just for having them in your possession, even if you don't read them.' It was all very well my protesting: 'I'm not a Communist, Father! But how can you criticise communism if you haven't read *Das Kapital*?' Obviously, such reasoning would not wash with the police.

My father said: 'Yes, I've kept them for you. The police pay no attention to an elderly and virtually unknown sculptor. But I don't want you to get arrested just for a piece of nonsense. I'd rather you were a pilot, in spite of the great dangers involved. Don't worry, I'll keep them for you. You can read them after your . . .'

He stopped suddenly. Perhaps he was going to say 'after your demobilisation'. My mother lowered her eyes, visibly saddened. Her heart was heavy.

'So much the better!' I said to cheer them up. 'I was going to suggest you sell them to buy some provisions. But, I must admit I shall be happy to find them waiting for me when I'm demobbed. . . . Besides, it might be difficult to find anyone willing to buy them just now. . . .'

I pronounced the word 'demobbed' eagerly, but of course they knew that I was lulling them with false hopes. They were not reassured. I myself never even dreamed of being alive when demobilisation came.

'Next time,' said my mother, 'I shall bring Nobuko. You haven't seen her since you enlisted.'

'Yes, Mother! That would give me immense pleasure.'

Nobuko was my second sister. God alone knew if I would ever have the joy of seeing her again. It was rumoured that we would be sent to a base in the Philippines early in April. My parents and I did not want to spoil the brief and fugitive happiness that we felt, so we kept our emotions well under control.

At 2200 hours on March 9, three blasts of the siren were followed by the announcement on the loudspeaker: '*Aka* three hundred and thirty. Stand by!' All the pilots leapt up and dived into their flying suits. We trainees had not yet begun our firing practice on the Ki-43, so we could only go out in the squadron's Ki-27s.

123

An hour later, a single blast on the siren! The loudspeaker spoke at once: 'Take cover in the air raid shelters!' Bitterly disappointed, we ran to the shelters. A heavy and threatening silence seemed to reign over the landscape. Towards one o'clock in the morning, a deep rosy colour tinged the sky to the south-east: the B-29s must have started bombing the capital. According to information from the commander of the defensive zone of Kanto, 334 planes had flown over at an altitude of 6,000 feet. At last, losing patience, one of the pilots spoke to our commanding officer in the darkness: 'Excuse me, sir, we would like your permission to make a sortie! It is time we took off . . . '

'No!' replied the C.O. sternly. 'I am just as frustrated as you are, but we have no orders. The Fifty-third Squadron based at Matsudo is responsible for destroying the bombers. Control yourselves!'

Were the buildings of the Imperial University of Tokyo, my university, on fire? We waited impatiently for news of the destruction of the Superfortresses. I could see again those giant craft that I had seen for the first time over Kyushu. Amongst them must be those I had allowed to escape. One o'clock . . . two o'clock. The time trickled away slowly. At last, at 0430 hours, the all-clear sounded. The B-29 raid had lasted for nearly three hours. Enraged at our enforced inaction, we went back to bed sullenly, without a word.

At 0800 hours, the voice of a Service Corps soldier attached to the cadet pilots made us jump. With our nerves on edge, we had only managed to doze, rather than sleep.

'Order from the commandant: training will begin at 0830 hours.'

After the night alert, we had expected to stay in bed till ten. But nobody made a murmur against the orders. Hurrying into our flying suits, we ran to the airstrip, where Flight Lieutenant Uehara was waiting for us in front of a Ki-43. He said solemnly: 'From now on, the enemy may possibly attack every day. Your training in firing from the Ki-43 is therefore more urgent than ever. We must take advantage of every moment of respite from American raids.'

The Ki-43 was equipped with a reflector sight, which showed the correct point of aim once your adversary was in the sight. The pilot only had to glance at it, which meant that he could retain his normal position, without having to move his head. He could also turn his eyes away and search the skies for other attackers, while still keeping his aim; this was vastly superior to the telephoto sights on the Ki-27, which obliged the pilot to place his eye against the lens each time he aimed, thus giving him little chance to watch out for enemies. In spite of this advantage, accurate firing was still difficult. In all positions, the plane had a tendency to side-slip at the moment of firing. It was only very rarely that a pilot could fire whilst flying level. All the cadet pilots acknowledged the fact that the period of training allowed to us would be quite inadequate. It was undeniable.

That evening, in the mess, one of the officers told us about the raid on Tokyo and described its horrifying effects. Taking off from airfields on the Marianas, Guam, Saipan and Tinian, and loaded with almost 2,000 tons of bombs, the B-29s had aimed for over three hours, not at military targets, but at the wood and paper houses of the densely crowded poorer districts of the city. This ensured the most efficient use of incendiaries. Unfortunately, our night fighters had been able to make only a feeble impact on the bombers: fourteen shot down and forty-two damaged. The poor quarters had been engulfed in flames within the blinking of an eye and most of the inhabitants burned alive. Rough estimates gave the figures as 270,000 houses burned, 85,000 dead and 40,000 wounded. [This was the most destructive single air raid in history; three hundred and thirty-four B-29s, flying at 7,000 feet, destroyed fifteen square miles of Tokyo. The author errs on the conservative side: in fact 100,000 people were injured. Editor.]

'My God!' exclaimed the officer. 'This must be the most gruesome spectacle ever witnessed. The streets are cluttered with charred corpses. Some of them died writhing in agony, you can see that from the positions of the bodies. It's a scene straight from hell!'

This savage raid shocked the nation beyond anything that had gone before.

Two nights later, my home town, Nagoya, was attacked by the B-29s. On March 13, it was the turn of Osaka, the second largest city in Japan. Incendiaries everywhere . . . probably my home no longer existed. The air raids went on. They were not aimed at military targets, but designed to provoke panic amongst civilians.

Ten days later, the American fighters invaded the skies over Kanto. We received no orders to sortie, so there we were, all the pilots of the 24th Squadron, forced to remain earthbound, grinding our teeth in rage and frustration. The enemy aircraft flew imperturbably over our heads, no higher than 3,250 feet. Eight . . . ten . . . fifteen planes! At that moment, I saw six Ki-61s (called 'Darting Swallows') pursuing the enemy. A few seconds later, they went into the attack, using aerobatic tactics. One plane caught fire just as it started to loop-the-loop. Was it an American or one of ours? 'It's one of ours!' someone shouted. As it fell in flames, we glimpsed the Rising Sun painted on the fuselage. The pilot parachuted out. The white balloon unfurled itself against the blue sky. Even in these circumstances, the contrast between the two colours was poetic. But beneath this white semi-circle, a human being was in mortal danger, and the thought wrung my heart. An enemy fighter circled round the parachute and fired several tracer bullets! He was machine-gunning his defenceless enemy. What cowardice! Was this an example of American chivalry? In my imagination, I pictured our pilot weeping before his head dropped forward abruptly. Our helplessness made my blood boil.

Our experienced pilots perished one after another. Our army could not regain mastery of the air over the territories occupied by the Americans. Yet the outcome of the war in the Pacific depended solely on supremacy in the air. Exceptional means were needed to salvage the situation. The military high command proposed the mobilisation of 1,900,000 men to aid in administration and improve supplies. Half the civilian motor cars and a number of horses would be commandeered. As well as this, it was hoped to organise an army of volunteers (men under sixty-five and women under forty-five), and a fighting force composed of men under sixty and women under forty – a total of some 28,000,000 people. So, my comrades Oshima and Suzuki would be called up, they would have to abandon their studies. I felt sorry for them.

But how were these newly mobilised forces to be armed when we were already short of ammunition? Reserves had been still further reduced by the American raids and the short-age of manpower. The situation was so serious that coins were now being struck in clay. The projected manufacture of 1,700 airplanes remained aleatory. In these critical circumstances, the military high command was considering limiting our defences to the landing beaches on the Japanese archipelago. Our navy wanted to mount a decisive battle off the shores of Okinawa, using the 3,700 planes which were to be sent to them as reinforcements before the end of April. They judged that an engagement off Okinawa would be more effective. However, it would be nothing more than a diverting action to gain time.

On March 16, the battle for Iwo Jima, begun on February 25, was to end tragically. General Kuribayashi, in command of the island's garrison, sent his last message to Tokyo: '... We have exhausted our ammunition and the last drop of water. The survivors of this hard battle are about to make a last assault against the enemy. We give thanks for the blessings and favour of His Imperial Majesty and we shall never regret sacrificing our lives for our country. The moment has come to say goodbye. . . . ' On March 27, the General shot himself in the head. His men fought to the death. The defeat was a mortal blow, for the capture of this island enabled the long-range P-51 Mustang fighter to escort the B-29. The war was entering its last desperate phase. It was out of the question for Japan to surrender without a struggle. The essence of *Bushido* was to fight on until one's sword was broken and one's last arrow spent. How could we find a way out of this extremely difficult situation? Ideally, it would be better to prevent the enemy planes from invading our skies, rather than concentrate on shooting them down once they were there, but it would be impossible to wipe out all the B-29 airfields in the Marianas, since we had lost both air and sea supremacy. At least we could try to stop the American fighters taking off from the aircraft carriers. This was how we came to consider suicide-attacks, since it was a matter of the utmost urgency to destroy the enemy carriers that dared to show themselves in our waters. But the use of this desperate means did not come about in a very direct manner.

A tardy spring was now approaching, but far from rejoicing, we felt that death was hastening his footsteps towards us. Suicide-attacks demanded technical skill of a very high order, and I had a feeling it was still too early for them to call on us to carry out such problematic missions. We were not sufficiently experienced, and the delays in our advanced training would prevent our inclusion in the suicide-squads.

Or was it that, at the bottom of my heart, I was really counting on that? In any case, this feeble hope, much to be deplored, gave way before my ardent desire to contribute to victory. I was torn by contradictions and railed at myself for faintheartedness.

127

The history of suicide-attacks dates from October, 1944.*
It was Takada, commandant of the 5th Army Squadron, who
first attempted this kind of attack. He had deliberately crashed
his plane on an enemy ship during the Battle of Biak Island,
at the end of May, 1944. And in mid-October, Rear Admiral
Arima's plane, damaged by bullets, had dived down in an effort
to strike an American carrier during the Battle of Formosa. It
fell into the sea close by without reaching the ship. However,
the suicide-attacks carried out by these two heroes were not
preconceived and planned. It was October 20 that the first
collective special attack squad was officially formed under the
leadership of naval Lieutenant Yukio Seki.

Nowadays, even in Japan, pilots of this special attack force
are usually called kamikaze, but during the war their official
name was *Shimpu Tokubetsu-Kogekitai* (Special Attack Corps)
in the navy and *Shimbu Tokubetsu-Kogekitai* in the army.
Shimpu means the Divine Wind and *Shimbu* the Gathering of
Courageous Forces. At the beginning, they were called
Tokubetsu-Kogekitai, or *Tokkotai* for short. They were never
called kamikaze, as they are today. Kamikaze also means the
Divine Wind. All Japanese characters have a double pronuncia-
tion: Divine Wind can be pronounced *Shimpu* or *kamikaze*.
The former is more dignified and solemn. Where, then, did the
form *kamikaze* come from? As far as I know, it was the *nisei*
in the U.S. forces who were the first to use it. Although they
were sons of Japanese fathers who had emigrated to the U.S.A.,
they did not know how to read Japanese correctly and so pronounced the two Japanese characters for Divine Wind in a
more vernacular way.

The first Special Attack Corps was born in the navy.

At the end of July, 1944, the 1st Naval Air Fleet was formed
under the command of Vice Admiral Teraoka. The previous
one had been totally destroyed. On August 12, when the Vice
Admiral arrived at Davao, on the island of Mindanao in the
Philippines, he had a total of about 300 aircraft at his disposal,
including several transport and reconnaissance planes. After
urgent demands to the high command, the number was in-

*The author recounts the history of the kamikaze operation from his
own experience, and also from articles entitled 'The Emperor in the History
of the Showa Era,' which appeared in the newspaper *Yomiuri* between
January 25 and February 14, 1967.

creased to 500, but of these, only 280 were capable of effective action.

On September 10, a sentry started a false alarm: 'Amphibious enemy forces in sight!' No one could believe his ears: the plane which had made a 400-mile reconnaissance over the sea the day before had reported nothing. Nevertheless, 100 fighters from Davao were hastily sent to the base at Cebu. The enemy's incessant patrols soon discovered our fighters massed on this small airfield, and they were not going to let such a marvellous chance pass by. Two days later, 160 planes attacked in several waves from 0900 hours till 1700 hours. Caught unprepared, almost all our fighters were destroyed, though they managed to bring down ten of the enemy. And, of course, losses from other attacks had to be taken into account also!

In effect, the 1st Naval Air Fleet possessed only thirty fighters when Vice Admiral Takijiro Onishi, the new commander-in-chief, arrived on October 17. Air Force planes were divided into three categories: those which were capable of engaging in air battles, those which constituted a reserve, and those in need of repairs. A total of thirty therefore meant only ten actively available. In spite of his high-sounding title of commander-in-chief of the 1st Naval Air Fleet, the Vice Admiral commanded barely a squadron. Having directed the administration of aeronautical armaments, he was well aware that he had not the slightest hope of receiving additional planes.

The 201st Fighter Squadron of the 1st Naval Air Fleet formed the first suicide-attack corps. It may be thought that this extraordinary procedure was born of despair, but it was not so. Pilots had long been deliberating on every possibility of destroying the Task Force with a limited number of fighters. The bomber squadrons were equally short of aircraft, but, for a single bomber in production, five fighters could be made. It was therefore on the latter that our aircraft industry concentrated. The logical consequence was to attack the Task Force solely with fighters. The pilots hit on the idea of loading their Zeros with one 550-pound bomb. Of course, one could not hope to sink an aircraft carrier with a single bomb of this type, but at least it could put the ship out of action by rendering the flight deck unusable. It would mean literally 'wave-hopping', skimming just above the water, then releasing the bomb in such a manner that it would hit the flight deck after bouncing off the surface of the sea. Various elements had to be calculated:

the altitude from which the bomb was dropped, the speed of the aircraft and its distance from the target, the direction of the wind, effects of rough or calm surface and so on.

The 201st Squadron began a training that proved to be full of hazards: for example, a bomb released at an altitude of thirteen feet rebounded to a height of sixteen feet and the airplane passed under the bomb! After practising at peril of their lives, the pilots concluded that it was necessary to drop the bomb from thirty feet and at a distance of 325 yards in order to reach the target. Another problem arose: how to avoid crashing the plane. The Zero fighter, with a top speed of 280 miles per hour, was in danger of crashing into the ship 2.4 seconds after dropping the bomb. No matter how skilful he was, the pilot had only one chance in a hundred of escaping. And anti-aircraft fire from the ships reduced this to 0.1 per cent. Vice Admiral Onishi personally reduced this safety margin to zero. On October 18, he had an interview with Vice Admiral Teraoka, who was leaving the base.

'Normal tactics are no longer valid,' said Teraoka.

'I agree with you entirely. If we really want to win, we must eschew all sensibility. I suggest we appeal directly to the pilots to carry out these suicide-missions, rather than go through their squadron leaders. Crashing our fighters against the aircraft carriers seems to me our last chance. What do you think?'

'All the same, I think it would be better to entrust the squadron leaders with this appeal to the men.'

'Very well! We shall call this suicide-attack corps *Shimpu Tokubetsu-Kogekitai*. It will be divided into four groups: *Shikishima* [Beautiful Island], *Yamato* [the Japanese people], *Asahi* [Rising Sun] and *Yamazakura* [Wild Cherry Blossom].'

These four names were suggested by an ancient Japanese poem:

> If you ask me what is the soul of the Japanese,
> The people of the Beautiful Island,
> I will tell you that it is the Wild Cherry Blossom
> That scatters its perfume in the light of the Rising Sun.

The blossom of the wild cherry, having scattered its perfume, falls without regrets. The meaning of this verse is that our people must always be ready to die for the benefit of their country, and, like the blossom, they must fall without regrets.

Next evening, Vice Admiral Onishi called five officers into a room in the headquarters of the 201st Squadron, which was based at Clark Field in the island of Luzon in the Philippines. Those present were Captain Inoguchi, senior General Staff Officer of the 1st Air Fleet, Captain Tamai, second-in-command of the 201st Squadron, naval Lieutenants Ibusuki and Yokoyama, who were senior pilots, and a Staff Officer of the 26th Squadron. He looked at them for a long time and then addressed them in a very grave tone:

'Kurita's fleet,' he said, 'is absolutely compelled to make a stand in the Gulf of Leyte. We are charged with giving him air cover. We must knock out the flight decks of the enemy carriers for a week at least. . . . In my opinion, the sole method of attack that could achieve this end is a suicide-attack led by Zeros loaded with five hundred and fifty pound bombs. What do you think?'

After a moment's silence, Tamai spoke: 'I am only the second in command, sir. Since it concerns the entire squadron, I feel I must seek the opinion of my superior, Captain Yamamoto,* before giving an answer.'

'I have already spoken to Yamamoto in Manila. You need have no hesitation in adopting his opinion.'

The truth of the matter was that Onishi had not yet discussed it with Yamamoto. His had indeed summoned him to Manila, but instead of waiting for his arrival, had impatiently taken off and flown to the 201st Squadron base. Having missed Onishi at Manila, Yamamoto set out to return to his base, but had to make a forced landing on the way. He was injured and taken to hospital.

Everybody understood perfectly well Onishi's impatience and irritation. Indeed, they shared it, but there was a subtle difference between spontaneous suicide-attacks and actually ordering men to sacrifice their lives. The circumspect Tamai, not knowing what to reply at once, asked the commandant for a few minutes to reflect, and to discuss it with his comrades. When this was granted, he left the room with Ibusuki.

The two men had an impassioned interview. They were concerned as to the effect this suicide order would have on the pilots. Their morale was high, but would they think such

*Captain Sakae Yamamoto, not to be confused with Admiral Isoroku Yamamoto, whose death occurred on active service in April, 1943. (*Translator's note.*)

an order justified? Everything would be determined by the first attempt: if it succeeded, and proved that a single fighter could effectively damage an aircraft carrier, then everyone would be willing to carry out similar missions; the order would vindicate itself. On the other hand, a failure would be disastrous, it would utterly demoralise the pilots.

Captain Tamai called together the N.C.O. pilots of the 9th Intake. They had come under his command a year previously, at the 263rd Squadron's air base at Matsuyama in Shikoku, and had shared with him in various battles from the Marianas to Yap. Two-thirds of them had been killed and there were only twenty-three survivors. Tamai explained Onishi's proposal. In the gloomy room, lit by a single bulb, he saw their eyes shining with enthusiasm! The twenty-three pilots replied simply and without hesitation: 'Right, we agree. No problem!' They were too young to express their feelings more articulately. Confronted with this burst of patriotic fervour, Tamai felt his eyes fill with tears. He went immediately to his commander's office to report his men's willing consent.

All that remained was to choose their leader. They would have liked to propose naval Lieutenant Sugano, an extremely brave officer who had distinguished himself during the Battle of the Yap Islands. Frustrated by the invulnerability of the B-24, he had rammed his plane into his foe and brought him down. Although half the wing was torn off his own plane, he had managed to return to base. He always kept his personal belongings in a little box labelled: 'Property left by the late Captain Tadashi Sugano.' He was bound to die heroically and so merit the posthumous promotion. Unfortunately, at that moment, he was in Japan collecting extra planes, and it was Tamai himself who had ordered him to go!

There were only about fifteen officers left in the 201st Squadron. To whom should they entrust this difficult and important mission, which would demand the highest qualities of its leader: honour, courage, outstanding ability and absolute levelheadedness? Tamai at once thought of naval Lieutenant Yukio Seki. He had come from Formosa only one month before, so Tamai did not know him as well as he knew Sugano. But he knew that he was Sugano's equal from the point of view of patriotic devotion and skill as a pilot. It was one in the morning. Tamai sent a sailor to awaken Seki, then went to wait for him in the mess, with Inoguchi. A few minutes later, he heard Seki's step on the stairs. He turned his head towards the door, where the lieutenant soon appeared.

'Present, sir!' he said, standing at attention.

Tamai invited him to sit beside him and tapped his shoulder before speaking. His throat was so constricted by emotion that he could barely get the words out. Understandably, he had difficulty restraining his tears: he had the exceedingly painful job of sending a twenty-three-year-old officer to certain death – and Seki had just got married! After a long silence, Tamai explained to him the purpose of Vice Admiral Onishi's visit, then declared: ' . . . and I have chosen you to lead the mission.'

Pale and tight-lipped, Seki remained silent, impassive. His elbows were resting on the table and he held his head in his hands. What was going through his mind at that moment? Was he thinking of his heavy responsibility? Or of his young wife? He was silent for so long – or so it seemed to Tamai and Inoguchi – that they began to wonder whether he would answer at all. In reality, it was only a few seconds later when he suddenly lifted his head and pushed the hair back from his forehead. (Naval officers were allowed to wear their hair long, whereas, in the army, it had to be close-cropped.) His interlocutors tensed with anxiety. With shining eyes, Seki looked into their faces and said: 'I beg you to entrust me with this mission.' There was no uncertainty in his voice, it expressed a firm resolution. 'Good,' said Tamai simply, unable to find words to express the profound appreciation that flooded his whole being. Inoguchi, the General Staff officer, left the mess hastily, as if afraid of showing his emotion.

The unnatural pallor of Seki's face disturbed Tamai. After all, wasn't this young officer entitled to ask him why he had thus been condemned to death? The anxiety showed on his face and Seki guessed his feelings.

'Please don't worry, sir,' he said almost joyfully. 'I have had diarrhoea for several days, that is why I look so pale.'

Tamai seemed relieved, as if he accepted the explanation.

After leaving the mess precipitately, Captain Inoguchi knocked on Vice Admiral Onishi's office door, eager to make his report. The latter was lying on his camp bed, waiting impatiently. When Inoguchi entered, he sat up abruptly.

'The choice has been made, sir,' said the captain. 'Lieutenant Seki, an ex-pupil of the Naval Academy.' Onishi nodded his head. 'Good!' He too seemed satisfied, though inwardly suffering anguish.

The night of October 19–20 passed slowly. The twenty-four pilots who had just been assigned to special attack missions, and the commander-in-chief, spent the night under the same roof, for the first time. The Vice Admiral could think of nothing but the tragic destiny that awaited these men. Conscious of the great weight of responsibility on his shoulders, he committed hara-kiri on August 16, 1945, after Japan had been defeated. There is a Japanese proverb which says: 'It is only after his death that one can estimate a man's true worth.' Onishi himself often said: 'Even when I am dead, people will hesitate to accord me my true worth. I shall never have a friend who understands me.' It is certainly true that no one will ever know what passed, that night, in the hearts and minds of Onishi and his heroic men.

The morning of October 20 was clear and fine. It was autumn, the season when man reaps what he has sown. For the twenty-four pilots of 201st Squadron, the fruits of their labour were their gruelling training and the sacrifice of their lives. Since dawn, they had been busily preparing for their mission. They were laughing, as if they had forgotten the dramatic resolution they had taken only a few hours before, and, to look at them, no one would have believed they were on the point of taking off on a mission from which they knew they would not return.

After breakfast, the enemy Task Force showed no signs of putting in an appearance. Vice Admiral Onishi took advantage of this respite to harangue his men. A kind of moral dread had seized his soul, and for once he dropped his high rhetoric and spoke in a voice full of sorrow and affection.

'My sons,' he said, 'who can raise our country from the desperate situation in which she finds herself? Not the ministers, not the political advisers to the Throne, nor the Naval Chiefs of Staff. Still less a humble commander-in-chief like myself! You alone, who have souls as pure as they are steadfast, you alone hold this power. That is why I have dared to ask you, in the name of one hundred million Japanese, to carry out this mission. I hope with all my heart that you may be successful, that you . . .'

He could no longer find the words. At that solemn moment,

the lightest word would have rung hollow. Onishi was trembling.

At 1500 hours, it was reported that the U.S. Task Force was located to the east of the island of Samar. The suicide-pilots wanted to take off without delay, but Onishi would not order a sortie yet. 'Look!' he said, pointing to a naval map. 'The distance to the enemy's present position is exactly that of the Zero's range, so they would have little chance of catching up with the Task Force. I cannot permit their departure. This mission *must* succeed at first strike, it can't be repeated.' A few minutes later, he left for Manila, where he hoped to persuade headquarters to defer Kurita's ships engaging with the Task Force until after the intervention of the Special Attack Corps. Unhappily, Kurita's 2nd Fleet had left their base two hours earlier and were already making for Leyte.

That same morning, no sooner was he up than a certain naval Ensign First Class Kuno noticed that an abnormal atmosphere pervaded the 201st Squadron's base. An ex-university student who had signed on at the naval flying school, he knew nothing of the formation of a *Shimpu* corps. He received orders to leave for Cebu airfield under the command of naval Captain Nakajima, the senior pilot. Preoccupied with preparations for departure, he had not even been aware of Onishi's harangue. Before leaving, he anxiously enquired of Nakajima what was going on at the base. But the latter only replied brusquely: 'Nothing!'

The formation of eight Zeros, led by Nakajima, left for Cebu at 1700 hours. Four of these Zeros belonged to the *Yamato* group; it had been decided to send them to Cebu and entrust Clark Field to three other groups. Being closer to the American carriers, Cebu was more exposed to danger, but it held one trump card: it was relatively difficult to spot from the air.

On landing, Nakajima mustered his pilots and told them that a suicide-attack corps had just been formed. Then he said: 'Others will want to follow in the footsteps of the first pilots charged with this mission. Volunteers should simply write their name and rank on a slip of paper and put it into an envelope. Those who do not wish to volunteer should submit a blank paper. The senior officer amongst you will bring me the envelopes before twenty-one hundred hours. No one but myself will know the outcome. I understand that each man has his

135

personal reasons for his decision, and I assure you that those who do not accept this mission will never be blamed for lack of patriotism.'

As the envelopes were placed in front of him, Nakajima felt his heart beat faster. What would he do if everyone had handed in a blank? At the moment of slitting the envelopes, he felt a due sense of awe, for he understood the sacredness of the thing. He opened each one with care. Only two blank slips! The two pilots who had handed these in were both suffering from serious illnesses. He sighed with relief. At that moment, Ensign First Class Kuno came into his office. His eyes were bloodshot and he looked angry.

'Excuse me, sir,' he said, hammering out his words, 'but I cannot understand how you can be so thoughtless as to exclude me from the suicide attack corps.'

'Oh, but you haven't been excluded at all,' replied Nakajima. 'You will be part of the group flying the Zeros we have just brought to Cebu.'

Kuno smiled. His whole expression cleared. He saluted and left the room, looking really happy. A few minutes later, Nakajima heard someone playing the piano. It must have been Kuno, for he was the only one at Cebu airfield who could play it well. Now, he was playing for the last time, and he put his whole soul into the music. Perhaps he was pouring out all his love for his wife. . . .

At 1500 hours on the 21st, a message was received: 'Enemy aircraft carriers sighted sixty nautical miles to the east of Suluan Island.' At that very moment, four Zeros of the *Yamato* group, together with two escorting Zeros, had just lined up on the runway. Several U.S. Grummans appeared in the sky over the field. In the winking of an eye, six Zeros were hit by bullets, though luckily their bomb loads did not explode, and they were too badly damaged to fly. If only we could follow the Grummans, we would be able to locate the enemy aircraft carriers exactly, which we had not so far been able to do, owing to the shortage of reconnaissance planes. Nakajima instantly ordered the preparation of the reserve aircraft. Ten minutes later, three more Zeros were ready. Kuno was in one of these. Nakajima said to him: 'You have no protective escort planes. If you cannot fulfil the mission, do not hesitate to turn back!'

'Don't worry,' replied Kuno, 'I shall certainly find some worthwhile targets at Leyte.'

That night, two Zeros came back, having failed to locate the carriers. Kuno's Zero did not return. According to an American communiqué, no aircraft carriers were damaged that day.

At Clark Field, the *Shikishima* group, commanded by Lieutenant Seki, was on constant readiness for a suicide-mission. On that same day, at 1900 hours, the message came in: 'Enemy carriers sighted east of Leyte.' Seki took off at the head of his flight of Zeros, after having consigned to Tamai's care a paper in which he had wrapped a lock of his hair. However, all the Zeros were obliged to return to base without having been able to find the U.S. Task Force. The *Shikishima* group made sorties on each of the three days that followed, but had to return frustrated every time.

On the 24th, the battleship *Musashi* had the misfortune to be sent to the bottom. Feeling that this was due to his failure to sight and destroy the enemy aircraft carriers, Seki bowed low before Tamai and said: 'I have no excuses.' Tamai saw tears streaming down his cheeks.

At 0725 hours on the 25th, the *Shikishima* group, composed of five bomb-loaded fighters and four escorting Zeros, left Clark Field. At 1040, the lieutenant's formation chanced upon some American aircraft carriers about 850 nautical miles off the island of Leyte. Seki waggled his wings as a signal to attack, dived, and skimmed just above the waves towards one of the carriers. Before the ship could begin evasive manoeuvres, or the anti-aircraft guns could open fire, he had crashed into the carrier, exactly between the flight deck and the hull. The bomb he was carrying exploded, making a huge hole in the side of the ship. Another Zero followed Seki and, with consummate skill, plunged into the hole already ripped open in the ship's side. The carrier fled, zigzagging as it went. Pilots in the other Zeros saw flames and black smoke billowing to a height of 3,000 feet. Another Zero crashed into a second carrier and set it on fire. Yet another hit a heavy cruiser, which belched smoke and was presently shaken by secondary explosions. The *Shikishima* group had finally carried out their suicide-mission! A horrifying spectacle, but, at the same time, a historic event. The heroes of this first suicide group had undoubtedly kept their eyes wide open right up to the fatal moment of the crash, as if they wanted to watch their own lives vanish forever.

This took place early in the afternoon. The airmen at Cebu Field saw a Zero approaching at top speed. Sometimes, damaged planes from other squadrons arrived unannounced in this manner. The base was famous for giving strangers a warm welcome, and all comers would be regaled with *sushi*. As a result, some pilots made 'forced' landings at Cebu just for the pleasure of indulging themselves with a plate of *sushi*! Thinking the Zero pilot must be one of these ravenous visitors, nobody paid any particular attention. The pilot made rather a wild landing and jumped out of his cockpit. He ran towards the commander's briefing room yelling: 'The *Shikishima* group have done it at last!' He was the pilot of one of the escorting Zeros. He gave Captain Nakajima a detailed account of the show put on by the heroic flyers. It was a tale to make one's hair stand on end. Nakajima immediately sent a message to H.Q.

'The *Shikishima* group of the *Shimpu* special attack corps have carried out a successful surprise attack on an enemy Task Force composed of four aircraft carriers, thirty sea miles northeast of Suluan Island. Two planes crashed into a carrier, which must certainly have sunk, the third started a fire on board a second carrier, and the last plane crashed into and sank a heavy cruiser.'

When Vice Admiral Onishi received this message, he was in conversation with Vice Admiral Fukudome, commander-in-chief of the 2nd Naval Air Fleet. They were speaking of this very mission. The 2nd Naval Air Fleet, possessing 500 planes, including reserves, arrived at Clark Field on the 23rd October. At a conference, Onishi proposed to Fukudome that he should form a special attack corps within his own body of men, but the latter refused. As I have already explained missions of this nature demanded highly trained pilots – normally, three years' training at a field base and five years on carriers would be considered necessary – and the Naval Air Fleet pilots had nowhere near this amount of experience. This was why Fukudome was against Onishi's proposal, although the two admirals continued to discuss the subject.

In 1951, I happened to meet Vice Admiral Fukudome, entirely by chance: I was acting as interpreter for a French journalist who was interviewing him. I took advantage of this to question him regarding the suicide-attack groups in his own Naval Air Fleet. I remember his replies exactly:

'At that period,' he said to me affably, 'I was sharing a

room in the headquarters of Two Hundred and First Squadron with Vice Admiral Onishi. He kept repeating that there was no other mode of action still open to us, and urged me to form similar corps in the Naval Air Fleet, which, by then, was non-existent except on paper. . . . Having no aircraft carriers left, we were perforce land-based. . . . But the fact was, my pilots were terribly inexperienced. En route for Clark Field, we attacked the U.S. Task Force off the coast of Formosa, and some of my pilots mistook dolphins for enemy subs! Others could not tell the difference between cruisers and destroyers. As an ex-kamikaze yourself, you will appreciate that this inexperience was an obstacle to the carrying out of such a difficult mission. On the twenty-fourth and twenty-fifth of October, we attacked the Task Force with all the means at our disposal. Result: two cruisers and three destroyers damaged. Need I say more?

'On the other hand, on the twenty-fifth, the *Shikishima* group carried off a brilliant success, sinking two ships, including the aircraft carrier *Saint Lo.* I spent the night of the twenty-fifth–twenty-sixth arguing with Onishi and finally promised him the support of all my Zeros. At dawn, I interrogated my staff officers. Some said this was now the only possible form of attack, others insisted we should try one more large-scale conventional attack. However, it had been drizzling since morning and in these conditions it would have been difficult to maintain flying formations. It was, therefore, circumstances that constrained me to take the final decision: I opted for special suicide-missions.'

The Emperor was immediately informed of the heroic, unprecedented death of these young flyers. Then the news was given to the nation. Three days after the success of the first suicide-attack, the words addressed by the Emperor to the Naval Chief of General Staff were transmitted to the front-line bases. Nakajima, pilot-in-chief of the 201st Squadron, assembled all pilots and mechanics and read them the message. Mounted on a little rostrum, he paused, then swallowed hard before speaking.

'I am going to read you the Emperor's words,' he said in a voice full of emotion. 'Here they are: "To think that it has come to this. . . . And yet, they have done nobly. . . . " '

Emotion nailed each man to the spot. Deathly silence. Everyone was thinking of what the Emperor must have felt in his heart when he heard this great news, and of the suffering that had shown in his face. With aching heart, he had graciously praised them, but wasn't his true feeling one of despair? When Vice Admiral Onishi read the message, he seemed to be seized with both respect and fear: he was conscious that his action, his decision as a leader, fully merited the criticism implicit in the Emperor's words.

On October 28, Admiral Toyoda, commander-in-chief of the Combined Fleet, presented a citation to the *Shikishima* pilots, and on November 12, their illustrious deeds earned them a promotion.

Thus, our aeronautical operation metamorphosed into a suicide-mission. After the navy, the army adopted the same tactic. It was in the Philippines that the 4th Air Force, under the command of General Tominaga, organised its Special Attack Corps, *Banda* (innumerable branches). During the Battle of the Philippines, the army lost 658 men on suicide missions. The navy invented this method by following through an irrefutable piece of logic: there was nothing else left to try.

We ordinary pilots, more or less experienced, suffered the vague presentiment that sooner or later we would receive orders to carry out suicide-missions. But we did not talk about it. Even when he is rushing towards disaster, man cherishes the insane hope that somehow he will survive. He comforts himself with the conviction that he will be the very last to fall victim to the tragedy.

March 31, 1945.

For some days now, the airmen had enjoyed walking up and down the avenue of cherry trees that joined the barracks to the large bathhouse; they were impatient to see the buds bursting forth, but this year spring was late. It was as if she was teasing us, deliberately withholding her favours.

One evening, I walked there in the twilight. Then I went to have a bath. As I entered our billet afterwards, someone said to me: 'Hey! Orders to muster at twenty-hundred-thirty. In the C.O.'s office!'

With his hands clasped behind his back, Commandant Suenaga walked up and down in front of the twenty-four pilots standing at attention. All the 1st Flight were present, and half the 2nd. The C.O.'s pale, tense face betrayed his agitation. The air was charged with anxiety. Suddenly, Suenaga stopped and looked at us one after the other. His gaze, gentle enough as a rule, seemed to transfix each man.

'As you know,' he said at last in a grave voice, 'the army is short of pilots, petrol, planes and ammunition . . . in fact, everything! We find ourselves at an impasse. There is just one last resort left to us: to crash on the decks of enemy aircraft carriers, as your comrades have done before you. Two hours ago, our squadron received the order to form a Special Attack Corps . . . I am compelled to ask you . . .'

He hesitated. But there was no need for him to go on. We knew at once that we were already committed. Of course, I had been expecting it, and yet, when I heard 'to crash on the decks of enemy aircraft carriers,' I could not prevent myself from shivering, as if I had been slapped in the face. These words struck me to the heart; my legs trembled, I could scarcely breathe. After a silence, the commander-in-chief went on:

'. . . to . . . to undertake this mission.'

It was an effort for him to bring out this phrase, which he hastily corrected:

'But of course you are free to choose. I will give you twenty-four hours to think it over. You will give me your answer tomorrow, before twenty hundred hours. You may present yourselves individually at my office.'

The words came out all in a rush. Perhaps he wanted to get this delicate subject off his chest once and for all. His face was contorted with emotion. He had said 'ask you' and not 'order you'. Now, in the army, a superior officer never asked, he simply ordered. This was truly exceptional. But then, even the most heartless officer would find it hard to ask his men to die. Military history teems with situations in which there was only a 10 per cent chance of survival, but one that left no possible chance at all was unique. It was really Suenaga's duty to order us, and he knew it. His distress was beyond anything imaginable.

'Well now,' he wound up, 'the squadron still needs pilots to fight off enemy planes that invade our skies. This will be the task of the second half of the Second Flight and the whole of the Third. I made my choice without ulterior motive, simply by numerical order. Dismiss!'

During the hour that remained before curfew, no one made any allusion to the C.O.'s instructions. All the same, we did not appear downcast: we chatted, laughed, put our personal belongings in order, just as usual. However, once we were in bed, I could tell that everyone was restless. Men were tossing and turning in their beds.

It was impossible to execute this highly skilful mission without special training, and the training could not last less than one month. One month to live! This thought delivered me from the obsessive idea of death. Human frailty makes us avoid looking death in the face. I said to myself: 'For the moment, sleep! Afterwards, your new life will begin . . . a life that leads directly to death. But, at this moment, your head is full of a thousand muddled reflections. They make no sense, so forget it . . . think about it later, at your leisure. . . . '

Suddenly, for no apparent reason, I began to worry about my right leg; it was still a little swollen, and I imagined my plane veering away just at the critical moment, as I was diving towards the target, because I had not been able to press the rudder pedal with my right foot. Upset, I tried to chase away this nightmare, then I started counting, a habitual remedy for sleeplessness since I was a child. Eight thousand . . . nine thousand . . . I do not know how many I counted. Sleep engulfed me like a deep chasm.

April 1.
I belonged to the 1st Flight. My fellow cadet pilots were, like me, willing to accept the commander's request. Perhaps we were influenced by the already tense and highly charged atmosphere of the base. In any case, deep down, we had been expecting it. Yet at the bottom of our hearts a vacillation, a reluctance of our whole beings, persisted. The C.O. had given us a free choice, not a categoric order. But, in the army, did an underling really have any choice but to say: 'Yes, sir! Certainly, sir!' to a superior officer? To obey orders and carry them out uncomplainingly is the fundamental duty of a soldier towards himself and towards the army. Therein lies the army's greatness and glory, as well as it inhumanity and ruthlessness. What would happen if soldiers refused to obey their officers?

For us, the question was something else: brothers have no need to ask one another to sacrifice their lives for the common defence. The security, the very existence of our families was threatened. Women, children and old men had already been among the innumerable and pathetic victims of bombing and machine gun fire. It was therefore natural that we should go to any lengths, regardless of our own safety, to protect our families. In a certain sense, our desire and the commandant's request coincided.

Referring to the circumstances in which our pilots joined the suicide-squads, it is often asked: 'Were they really volunteers, or acting on official orders?' I have no intention of glorifying this event, unique in the history of war, but as a witness who survived, I can affirm that our own wishes were in perfect accord with orders from the high command. It was so in my own case, at any rate, and presumably in the case of Lieutenant Seki. On the evidence, whole groups of aviators presented themselves for these missions, under pressure of urgent circumstances; on the other hand, no one but the man himself can claim to know the state of his soul. Regrettably, there are intellectual hypocrites in Japan today who make this claim, and indulge in censure of the kamikaze. The author of *Chiran*, for example, writes: '. . . If Lieutenant Seki reflected for a long time before replying, perhaps it was because he was devoured by anguish. Is it not true to say that, under the circumstances, it was not so much a voluntary act as a compulsory one? In the majority of cases, these pilots were "forced volunteers". Many veteran soldiers believe that the suicide corps represented the flower of the Japanese race, and that this worthy act was in the true tradition of our people.' (Page 337.)

Volunteers or conscripts: that is not the question. I can only reaffirm that all my comrades were ready to accept the order voluntarily, even to ask to be sent on a suicide-mission. It matters little whether they volunteered or acted under strict orders: their one thought was to defend their homeland, even at the sacrifice of their lives.

We ate our breakfast in the mess. Suddenly, Cadet Pilot Tanaka spoke up: 'Look, we're all ready to accept this mission. Why don't we go to the C.O. straightaway and tell him so?' Everyone agreed: 'Right!' We were already on our feet when someone said, by way of a joke: 'We might as well finish our breakfast, at least!' We all sat down again. I took advantage of this delay to bring up a detail:

'Our planes will carry a five-hundred to five-hundred and fifty pound bomb, so we shall have to make them lighter by stripping off the machine guns. And now we're so short of planes, we will not be given escort fighters, as the other special attack groups were. How, then, can we give the American

143

fighters the slip and get through to our targets? We must think about this. . . . '

'Think about what!' shouted Tanaka. 'You're an excellent pilot, what are you afraid of? Don't you want to accept the mission, don't you believe it can succeed?'

He looked at me sternly, leaned back in his chair and crossed his legs. A graduate of a Buddhist university in Kyoto, his character was cool and well balanced. Yet, at that moment, I sensed some change in him; he seemed tense, I had never seen him so worked up before.

'You pour scorn on what I say,' I replied, 'but my point is precisely this: suicide-attacks are the only method left to us, and therefore they *must* succeed. If, with our twenty-four planes, we can sink eight or nine enemy carriers, it will give time for the pilots who follow us to undergo full training. I am always ready to give up my life for the defence of Japan, but surely it is worth considering the best means of reaching the target. If we fail, if we allow ourselves to be shot down by ack-ack or American fighters, our sacrifice will serve no purpose.'

'By the way,' one of the cadets said suddenly, 'during the last month, I have noticed that my eyesight is failing. I cannot see the target clearly. I am doubtful about taking part in this attack.'

'Theoretically, the first man to spot the enemy wins the battle,' I said. 'But this mission does not necessarily demand such good eyesight, since our target will not be a plane but a huge aircraft carrier. All you have to do is follow the plane in front of you. Crashing won't be difficult. . . . '

'Nagatsuka's right up to a point,' said Tanaka, 'but I still think poor eyesight is fatal to a pilot. How will you be able to evade attacking fighters? I advise you to tell the C.O. the truth and let him decide what you should do. Have you consulted the M.O.?'

'Not yet,' replied the cadet. 'I didn't dare, in case he grounded me. I want to be a pilot right up to the end, you understand.'

He let out a deep sigh, full of sorrow, and lowered his eyes. His face expressed a profound bitterness. Suddenly, he put down his chopsticks, stood up and walked over to the window. After a few moments, he turned round, making a little woe-begone gesture.

'Well, it can't be helped,' he said. 'I'll tell the commandant the truth about my eyes. I hope he'll let me stay with you, that is my one wish!'

Flying Officer Enomoto came into the mess. He was our senior, a *tokuso* of the 1st Intake. He had studied Japanese history at Hiroshima High School. We stood up and saluted him. He returned the salute, then sat down with us. He looked intensely worried. Mastering himself with an effort, he said: 'You've decided, eh? Haven't we intellectuals a duty to fulfill after the defeat? Life too has its value. I thought it over last night. . . .'

'So,' said someone sarcastically, 'you're convinced that Japan will be defeated?'

'Yes and no! I have a distinct foreboding, but I can't answer that question clearly. The military high command doesn't always keep us informed of the real state of the war. . . . But, in life, it's no use giving in to despair, one must try to find a solution. No man wants his country to be vanquished. The government and the fighting forces have to take responsibility in this crisis. The civilians are in no way responsible, yet they are exposed to the risk of death! It is our duty, as pilots, to protect them at all costs. My personal life counts for nothing in comparison with the well-being of our people. I am going to say "yes" to the commandant.'

'Sir,' said Tanaka, 'we have all come to the same conclusion. Victory or defeat, that is no longer the question. Other suicide-pilots will follow us. This special mode of attack, and the number of carriers we manage to sink, cannot fail to impress the Americans. Even if these missions cannot ensure our victory, they will at least put us in an honourable position to negotiate an eventual armistice. . . . We are ready to go to the commanding officer with you.'

He looked round at his comrades. No one made any objections. We hastily gulped down our breakfast, then, led by Enomoto, we went to Suenaga's office. 'Sir,' said Enomoto, 'on behalf of these six cadet pilots of the First Flight, and myself, I request the favour of being sent on a special attack mission.' 'Thank you,' said the C.O. simply. Then, with his hands behind his back, he went and gazed out over the vast view from the window. Perhaps he did not want us to see that his eyes were misty with tears.

'Really,' he went on in an emotional voice, without turning

round, 'I cannot find words to thank you. You are students, not professional airmen. Your steadfastness and courage overwhelm me. Apart from one N.C.O. in the Second Flight, who is ill, every one of you has volunteered. . . . From this moment, special training will begin. Flight Lieutenant Takagui will be in charge of you.'

We walked out of the office, leaving behind the pilot who had complained of his eyesight.

At 0930 hours, just as we were about to start training, the air raid warning sounded. The B-29s had reportedly left their base, though their objective was not yet clear. In any case, the possibility of a raid prevented our taking off.

That same evening, our group was officially named 'Kikusui group of the Jun-no Special Attack Corps.' Kikusui denotes chrysanthemums floating on a river and Jun-no the sacrifice to the Emperor. In all, we were twenty-two pilots. The unlucky cadet who had been suffering from poor eyesight was rejected on these grounds, in spite of his eagerness to join. Inevitably, he was transferred to the non-flying personnel. His sorrow was apparent, whereas we, who were destined to die in a month or so, were full of high spirits.

April 2, 1945.
In theory, our training would be completed in thirty days. However, delays due to shortage of fuel, and to American raids, meant it could last as long as two months. We were therefore given priority, to the detriment of other pilots.

At 0730 hours, the order to begin training was given. Flight Lieutenant Takagui spoke solemnly to the twenty-two pilots gathered under the awning over the briefing room:

'I am in command of the Kikusui group. Training will begin with take-off practice. Later, we shall go on to simulated attacking dives with a ship as target: this awning will act as the target. At an altitude of sixteen feet, you will elevate the nose of the plane. Above all, do not shut your eyes at the last moment, that is absolutely vital. I am going to give you a demonstration.'

Takagui was twenty-three years old and a graduate of the Army Flying School. Very keen, with sparkling eyes, he sometimes gave the ground crews a rocket. Everyone was afraid of him, but he never ill-treated the pilots. It was said that he had shot down more than fifteen enemy aircraft during the Battle of the West Pacific. Tall and robust, he reminded us of a bronze statue. His face was rather inexpressive and he never smiled. In short, he was the very personification of the fanatical and shortsighted professional serviceman. But the thought that I was soon to share his fate, whether I liked it or not, made me look at him in a rather more sympathetic light.

There is a tendency to think that suicide-attacks were simply a matter of crashing blindly and heedlessly into the target. As I have already said, it was not as easy as that. Taking off, for example, required the utmost caution. With a bomb weighing over 500 pounds, the Ki-43 would stall if pulled off the ground in the usual way, so our first day was devoted to take-off drill. A log weighing about 200 pounds was fastened under the planes in lieu of a bomb. Needing a longer runway than the Ki-45 Kai, we had to bring the nose up right at the end of the airstrip, at the level of the trees that bordered the field. It was impressive to see the branches, from close to, bending in the wind produced by the plane. The undercarriage could not be retracted until we had gained sufficient speed, at a height of about 150 feet.

An hour later, take-off practice ended: we had to economise on fuel. The *Kikusui* group was composed of eight N.C.O.'s, ten cadet pilots and three junior officers, originally in the infantry, who had become pilots. There was a certain amount of implicit rivalry among the various pilots, but, oddly enough, once training began, a mutual sympathy drew them together; no doubt it was a sense of solidarity in face of a common destiny, as when all the rams in a flock close ranks in self-defence.

That evening, in the mess, Flight Lieutenant Uehara explained a suicide-attack to us in detail:

'You haven't read the papers for a long time,' he said, 'so you haven't heard about the success of the Second *Mitate* [Sacred Shield] group off Iwo Jima. Twenty suicide-planes heroically attacked the American ships escorting the troops who landed there on the twenty-first of February. Three suicide-planes crashed one after the other into the aircraft carrier, *Saratoga*, hurling themselves at the same point on the deck. She was forced to withdraw, badly damaged, and with more than two hundred dead and wounded. Another suicide plane hit the escorting carrier, the *Bismark Sea*, which sank after the crash had set off a number of explosions. Another escorting carrier and two transport ships were struck by other suicide-planes and suffered considerable damage. Our attack sowed terror amongst the enemy sailors, proving that this method has a certain psychological value. At the same time, it must be admitted that half our suicide-planes were caught by ack-ack as they dived and fell into the sea without reaching their objectives. Some, it is said, were hampered by jets of water thrown up by shells. The enemy have invented a new tactic: they explode shells all round their own ships so as to create a screen of water spouts . . . whatever you do, don't lose your heads, keep calm. If you are shot down during your crash-dive, you will die in vain. In the case of a water-skimming approach, you run the risk of being caught in the water spouts, as well as by the ack-ack. If you use the high-altitude approach, enemy fighters may shoot you down. Success is, either way, problematic. It is up to you to decide, by calmly calculating all the factors of the actual conditions present, whether to use the wave-hopping or the high-altitude approach.'

We realised how difficult our task was. Failure would be irredeemable, since the price of a single attack would be our lives. Moreover, it was not expedient for five or six suicide-planes to hurl themselves at the same ship. 'One plane against one ship,' that was the basic principle, Uehara's lecture gave me much food for thought.

April 4.
After take-off training, we tried the high-altitude approach for the first time. Today, April 4, was the fourth day of the fourth month of the year. Four is pronounced *shi*, and so is the word meaning death. The sound has a double meaning. I am not superstitious, but I could not prevent myself from reading omens everywhere: this training would lead me to my death in the very near future.

For the light fighters, two methods of approach had been developed: the high and the very low altitude. The former had the advantage of making interception by enemy fighters difficult. It consisted in concealing oneself amongst the clouds till the last possible moment, then starting the dive from 16,000 to 20,000 feet. At the end of the trajectory, the nose of the plane had to be pulled up to an angle of forty-five to fifty-five degrees in relation to the point aimed at. There could be only one attempt at this approach. In practice, I did not dive steeply enough at the beginning of the descent, and so passed high over the awning, which was supposed to be the aircraft carrier, instead of almost skimming it! Total failure. This brought home to me the realities of the problem.

Before dismissing us, Flight Lieutenant Takagui, still wooden-faced, said to us:

'In the case of the high-altitude approach, you should aim at the lift cages at the bow or the stern of the carriers. They present the weakest spot. Ideally, one should plunge down the funnel, it's the best way to sink a ship in the twinkling of an eye. But good God, if the experiment you just carried out had been real, you would all have fallen into the sea without striking your target. So we must go back and spend some time practising take-off and getting into formation with the minimum possible delay. Circling about over the airfield only wastes fuel!'

On April 1, the Americans landed on Okinawa, an island that forms part of metropolitan Japan. Our navy was to mount a decisive battle in this zone. Perhaps large numbers of suicide planes would be used in an effort to destroy the 5th U.S. Fleet. Some of the officers in our squadron were hoping that the Special Attack Corps' remarkable success would put an end to hostilities. The Battle of Okinawa marked a turning point in the destiny of Japan. And it is only 460 miles from Okinawa to Nagasaki. I was preoccupied with the question: would I be able to acquire sufficient technical skill to make a perfect suicide-attack before the battle was over?

April 11.
Since the 4th, training had been suspended due to lack of fuel. Early in the afternoon, as I sat writing up my diary in the cadets' quarters, someone suddenly shouted: Salute!' I jumped up and saluted an officer in a flying suit who was standing in the doorway. He wore a flight lieutenant's insignia on the left side of his chest. Taking off his helmet, he said: 'Everybody well?' It was Flight Lieutenant Fukushima, former leader of the 2nd Flight at Utsunomiya Flying School.

'Well, now,' he continued with his perpetual smile, 'are you making good progress with your flying? I came via this airfield to see you all, or rather, to say goodbye. I'm on my way back to Chiran base, then I'll soon be off again to crash my plane on enemy shipping near Okinawa . . . yes, a suicide-mission! And I envy you, you will fly the Ki-43, whereas I'll have to use the old reconnaissance aircraft, Type 99 [Ki-51]. It has a range of over three thousand miles, but the fixed undercarriage makes it even more obsolete than your Ki-43. . . . I'm leaving in a quarter of an hour. If you like, I can show you two methods of approach for suicide-attacks.'

Not a trace of anxiety on his face: neither excitement nor fear of death. He spoke with the utmost calm. One would have thought he was about to leave on an ordinary training flight. Was this last flight just a joy-ride to him? I thought more about what his wife and family would suffer than about what he himself felt.

On the way to the airfield, I asked him for news of Cadet Pilots Watanabe and Kagawa.

'Watanabe is at the base on Formosa, Kagawa's in Korea,' he replied. 'As they are closer to Okinawa than you are, they'll probably carry out their suicide-missions before you do.'

So I would never see them again. I recalled Watanabe's ever-smiling face and Kagawa's serious air with a good deal of nostalgia.

Before climbing into his Ki-51, Flight Lieutenant Fukushima tapped each of us on the shoulder, saying: 'Goodbye! Our next meeting will be at the Yasukuni Temple!' This was a reference to the Shinto temple where all soldiers killed in battle are honoured. 'See you at Yasukuni Temple!' was the slogan of Japanese soldiers.

'Good luck!' His plane took off and climbed steeply into the clouds. A few seconds later, he dived from an altitude of 13,000 feet, heading for the end of the aerodrome. He came down like an arrow. At a height of 15 feet above the runway, he lifted the nose of the plane and began clod-hopping. As he approached the briefing room, he waved his left hand without turning his head towards us. A last farewell! His plane flew as smoothly as if it were running on a rail. After skimming along the length of the runway, he climbed steeply again. We were all astounded at his skill. In the sky to the west, his plane, diminishing rapidly, waggled its wings and faded away. We were never to see him again.

We gazed at the sky for a moment without a word.

April 20.
The last birthday of my life! I could not help pondering on the deep affection with which my mother had surrounded me for twenty-one years. Her great, her only joy was to watch

over my growing up, and take endless pains for me. Nothing could take the place of this joy. In my body were assembled all those irreplaceable human qualities: maternal love, scientific knowledge, intelligence, reason, judgement. The death of my body would entail that of its innumerable cells and, at the same time, the total annihilation of these precious gifts. With my physical death, all my mother's loving efforts for my education would be reduced to zero.

War, of course, is no respecter of things: if an age-old tree is in the way of the firing line, a young officer will order it to be cut down without giving it a second thought, though, to the lovers who have vowed undying love beneath its branches, this tree is precious as a souvenir of their devotion. Sentiment has no place in battle. Romance, the beauty of nature – nothing exists in face of the necessity to carry off a victory. That is the inhumanity, the atrocity of war.

Nevertheless, we had made a firm resolve to sacrifice our lives for our homeland and our families, without indulging in sentimentality. I detest those pacifists who hypocritically claim to be patriots, though they do nothing but talk, instead of acting. Only action and a contempt for death can reconquer peace, once it has been shattered. Words really serve no purpose.

These false patriots constantly reproached our leaders for their incompetence. I must admit that the latter failed to take the necessary action, though they were always exhorting the people verbally. All this had its effect on the young suicide-pilots. One of our men had said recently: 'These hypocritical pacifists want peace only to save their own skins, though they are quite happy to sacrifice ours. Have they ever given a thought to our point of view, our feelings?'

People told us, however, that the Emperor never missed an opportunity to express his gratitude. Our commandant had told us that the Emperor had not allowed New Year to be celebrated in the customary manner. Usually, the high military leaders, in full-dress uniform, and members of the government went to the Imperial Palace to render homage, but not this year.

At midday, one of the military chamberlains had brought him a white wood tray on which were placed a bowl of *sekihan*, a grilled bream and a flask of *saké*. A meagre repast. He said respectfully to the Emperor: 'Your Imperial Majesty, this is the

151

meal offered to the suicide-pilots just before their heroic departure.' The Emperor looked at it in silence, making an effort to restrain his deep sorrow, but his eyes were bathed in tears. He stood up abruptly and left the room without touching the food. For an hour, all alone, he walked up and down in the garden, which was neglected and overrun with weeds. Undoubtedly, he was meditating on the future of his country, as well as on the authentic patriotism of the suicide-pilots.

The commandant concluded: 'This year, no one rendered homage to the Emperor, except the souls of the suicide-pilots. . . . '

April 29.
The Emperor's birthday. I went to Tokyo on leave. I would have liked to go to Koga to see my uncle's family, but the train service was very poor and I had not the time. As the train rolled slowly through the capital, I was horrified to see the effects of American bombing: it had been terribly efficient. Whole districts were reduced to cinders. Amongst the scorched ruins, I could make out nothing but little shacks built of planks and covered with zinc. A few citizens were fanning wood fires, on which they had placed small portable stoves, beside their huts. Charred trees looked like skeletons and seemed to embody the last cry of the victims. There must have been cherry trees amongst them. I thought for a moment of the lovely cherry blossoms that I would never see again. Three weeks ago, I had admired the avenues of blossom at the aerodrome. It was the very symbol of the brief life of suicide-pilots. I hummed the song called 'Flowers of the Same Cherry Tree', which my friends and I had sung as we walked down the avenues arm in arm.

> Flowers of the same cherry-tree, you and I
> Bloom in the courtyard of the same squadron.
> Opening our petals on the same day,
> So shall the day we fall be the same;
> We are destined to scatter our sweet blossom
> Bravely, and together, for our country.

Passengers on the train travelling to the west of Tokyo (where Saga had his house) looked very weary. Their faces were no more than masks, unsmiling and with the bloom of freshness gone. Helpless spectators of the struggle that was

152

crushing our country. Their miserable expression, like the life-less landscape, so bleak and grey, appealed dumbly for protection, reinforcing my desire to help them rediscover their humanity. No matter how ardently he wishes to fight, an infantryman's role in the battle is limited, whereas I, as a pilot, had the possibility of sending an enemy vessel to the bottom, all by myself! That was really something.

For us, the American fighters were like dangerous microbes: we had to exterminate them one by one and wipe out their breeding ground, the aircraft carriers.

An hour later, I found myself in front of Saga's house, which, by good luck, had not been destroyed. This particular district had not suffered too badly. I would have liked to see Saga's mother again, but the family had already been evacuated to a village at the foot of Mount Fuji. An old servant was taking care of the house. Saga was still studying medicine at Nagasaki. The housekeeper was kind enough to offer me a cup of green tea. Afterwards, I went back to the station, knowing no one else in Tokyo.

Standing on the platform of the North Station, waiting for the train to Kagohara, I struggled with the braid on my sword belt, which had come loose. An elderly and distinguished lady, accompanied by a young girl, came up to me and said in a friendly voice: 'Allow me to help you, Officer.' After fastening the braid, she looked at my pilot's insignia and asked: 'Were you at university?'

'Yes, madam,' I said, and thanked her warmly.

I could not take my eyes off the young girl, who was evidently her daughter. She had pretty features. Jet-black silky hair fell to her shoulders. A melancholy look passed over her face, perhaps adding to her beauty, which left me marvelling.

'This is my daughter,' said the lady. 'She has lost her only brother, a naval suicide-pilot. He was killed in February. We have just come back from the cemetery where he is buried. He was at the University of Tokyo, a student, like you . . . you remind us of him. We think of him constantly and my daughter cannot get over his loss. Like my son, you will one day swoop down in your suicide-plane. For us, you are one of the guardian angels. I wanted to express my gratitude, in the name of all the people.'

With tears in their eyes, they bowed low before me. A guardian angel! If an officer of the General Staff had used such an expression, it would have seemed just another platitude, but, in this case, my spirit was set on fire. I understood the accuracy of Admiral Onishi's reasoning when he said that the safety of our country could only be entrusted honourably to the suicide-pilots. I watched mother and daughter disappear among the crowd. In my heart, I vowed to sacrifice my life for them and for my country.

In the train the sorrowful eyes and regular features of the unknown girl would not leave me. She must be a person of great intelligence and faithful heart – just such a young girl as I had hoped to marry. She would have given me a healthy son, daring, honest and clever. The three of us would stroll along the river banks, as I had often done with my parents when I was a child. The poetry of nature would draw us ever more closely together. At night, when I lingered late at my work table, my wife would bring me a cup of hot tea, just as my mother used to. Alas! This idyllic dream would never be realised, for I was soon, and infallibly, to die. Yet I indulged this dream of future married life, giving free rein to my imagination, until the train pulled into Kagohara station.

April 30.
In a simple ceremony, all the cadet pilots were promoted to the rank of flying officer. We changed our insignia and our flying suits were decorated with gold braid on the sleeves. We were not particularly excited about our promotion. Tanaka said, jokingly: 'We shall be flight lieutenants in a month! The time will soon pass!'

Later that morning, we recommenced our suicide-attack training: the wave-hopping approach. Flight Lieutenant Takagui gave us a demonstration.

As I was climbing into my plane, an N.C.O. mechanic said to me: 'One of the cylinders is spluttering, sir, I think the trouble is in the ignition, I'll change the spark plugs.' 'Thanks,' I said, 'but there isn't time. I'll check it myself.' I gave the engine full throttle, it did not splutter. 'Well, I hope it's nothing serious,' I said, and took off.

Skim the ground, zoom climb to 10,000 feet; sight the target, dive, clod-hop again at a height of 650 to 750 feet. This very low altitude approach demanded a certain dexterity, but it was not so difficult as the high-altitude approach. It made it easier to escape radar detection but posed another problem: how to

154

pass unscathed through the screen of water spouts all round the enemy ship. There was another danger, whichever approach you chose, and that was that the pilot would close his eyes instinctively just before the moment of crashing. It was the most ticklish point. Our C.O. and Flight Lieutenant Takagui kept insisting on it and warned us repeatedly not to close our eyes. If we did, we would probably miss the target, especially since we would then be at maximum speed. We *must* avoid throwing our lives away in vain.

When the training session was over, a letter was brought to me in the officers' sitting room. It was from Flying Officer Fujisaki. He had written from Chiran Field in southern Kyushu: '. . . These days, suicide-attack groups go out almost daily against the enemy carriers off the shores of Okinawa. In a few days, it will be my turn. Frankly, I think this situation is the outcome of incompetence and stupidity on the part of the high command: it seems they are relying solely on the eager devotion of the young now. Suicide-pilots also have a symbolic value. It was not the young, however, who started the war. It is as if our leaders had broken off the writing of a novel they had started and which, for lack of inspiration, they are incapable of finishing. They are leaving it to the young men to bring it to a conclusion, but the young are not fully conversant with the plot! In a sense, we are scapegoats. What is the use of complaining? We are obliged to carry out the orders they impose on us. You and I are atheists. We shall never again have the pleasure of seeing each other, not even in the Great Beyond of believers. I hope that you will carry out your suicide-mission successfully. Good luck and goodbye forever!'

Fujisaki was about to die for his country. We had just heard news of the heroic death of Flight Lieutenant Fukushima: on April 16, he had taken part in a suicide-operation and had not returned to base. A pilot of his remarkable skill must surely have succeeded in striking an enemy ship. Had he kept that perpetual smile on his lips right up till the last moment? Promoted to squadron leader, he was no longer in this world. Where, then, was his soul? Fujisaki would answer: 'Not the least trace of it remains anywhere in the universe, nor is it in some imaginary Beyond.'

I have never been able to believe in reincarnation, like the Buddhists. If it were true, one would have to admit that my soul, once it had passed beyond this earthly life, would see my father, mother and sisters living here below, but without being able to address one word to them or let them know of my existence; what torture that would be! Far from plunging me into despair, the idea of oblivion soothed me. Matter born of nothingness, to nothingness man returns. Fundamentally, this is rather comforting. Being and nothingness, that was all. For me, there could be no middle way.

April 7.

The battleship *Yamato,* an enormous floating fortress and the pride of our navy, was sunk off Okinawa [On April 7, 1945. Editor]. The giant dreadnought, as well as the light cruiser *Yahagi* and eight destroyers, had been brought in by the navy to act as veritable bastions off the coast. These ships, like the suicide-planes, had only sufficient fuel for the one-way voyage. Every one of them was sunk or damaged, a tragic end for our Combined Fleet. The operation had certainly been daring, but it was also rash and ill considered. Henceforth, deprived of naval support, our army had no other resource but its suicide-planes. The evolution of the war now depended solely on the patriotism of these young fliers.

May 17.

After flying in formation for an hour, I saw our airfield through the clouds. It looked very small, like a matchbox. Before beginning the descent, I inspected the sky: no more enemy planes, they had raced away after machine-gunning the hangars and the living quarters of the base.

I pushed the stick slightly forward. The nose dipped, the plane lost height, then roared through the clouds which had helped the American fighters to conceal themselves and get away. Fulminating against heaven knows what, I pushed the stick still further forward and cursed the clouds: they had acted as enemy accomplices and now made our landing hazardous. I shouted at them: 'Blasted clouds, disperse! To hell with you!' The plane was losing altitude . . . 1,000 feet . . . 650 . . . 300 . . . landing. The grasses bent flat The airfield looked incredibly peaceful, like a lush green garden. Suddenly, I was overcome with fatigue and the need to rest. My comrades were landing in their turn. I regained my breath and taxied over to a corner of the field, in the opposite direction from the hangars, which were too exposed to danger. We had to keep our precious suicide-planes in the revetments in the forest. The engine stopped, my plane was stowed away, yet I had not the energy to climb out of the cockpit. I was the victim of an overwhelming apathy. It was certainly not the flight that had tired me, no, sir! For a fighter pilot, an hour's flying is nothing. Besides, I had not been engaged in combat. It was rather the humiliation I felt precisely because I had *not* engaged in a dogfight. Our aim now was not to shoot down the enemy, but to preserve our few planes intact, for our squadron had only twenty-five, mostly Ki-27s.

Since the beginning of April, at the sound of the alert, we had to fly as far as the coast. The machine guns had already been removed from our fighters and we did not even have any bullets. In short, our only job was to run away until ordered out on a suicide-mission, and this running away was deeply humiliating.

Peasants who lived around the base would wave their hands when they saw us taking off, convinced that we were going to repulse and shoot down the American fighters that threatened them. One morning, a rather ancient peasant had met me on a path not far from the base. He stopped and saluted grandly.

'Good morning, Officer,' he said. 'You are going to annihilate these wretched planes that hinder our work in the fields. We farmers know how brave you are. Good luck to you, and keep your courage up!'

Suddenly, I remembered his words. What a coward I felt! But what can one do with an unarmed fighter? Obsessed by this lack of means with which to hit back, a certain repugnance took hold of me . . . I no longer even thought of getting out of my plane. I closed my eyes.

A few seconds later, a group of young girls brought me back to my senses. Perhaps they were taking shelter in the forest. I jumped to the ground and approached them in the vain hope of rediscovering the girl I had seen at Tokyo station, and who was constantly in my dreams. Obviously, a chimera! These little girls had a frank and open air. Looking at them, I said to myself yet again: 'They need peace on earth! It is our responsibility to bring it about. I shall not regret my death if my sacrifice enables these children to enjoy a peaceful existence once more. . . .'

At the end of the afternoon, I received a letter from an N.C.O. at Chiran Field: 'I have the honour to announce to you the glorious death of Flying Officer Fujisaki at sea off Okinawa, on May 11. He was leading the 71st Flight of the Special Attack Corps. I am attached to the radiocommunications office. Before his departure, he told me he would transmit his wife's first name, in Morse code, instead of the usual signal. I listened attentively, and I distinctly heard the name of his wife transmitted by radio. I am convinced he made a successful crash dive. He often used to say he would have liked a more up-to-date and efficient plane, so as to be sure of succeeding. The truth is, most of these obsolete suicide-planes are defective. . . .'*

As a general rule, only the flight leader's plane was equipped with a radio. He would send the message: 'Attacking with all my planes' after signalling '. . . –,' then press the key down and keep it down until the last moment. Whoever was listening counted the number of seconds to judge whether or not he had succeeded in crashing. We had no other means of verifying

*I give here the statistics concerning suicide-planes engaged in the battle of Okinawa. They are taken from Takushiro Hattori's *General History of the Battle of the Pacific:*

Date	Navy	Army	Total
March 3 – April 3	106		106
April 4, 6, 7	209	146	355
April 12, 13	104	98	202
April 16	145	51	196
April 21, 22	69	62	131
May 4	112	84	196
April 4 – May 4	462	199	661
May 11	64	40	104
May 24, 25	98	5	103
May 27, 28	46	39	85
June 3, 7	15	31	46
June 21, 22	68		68
May 11 – June 22	77	179	256
June 23 – August 16	62		62
Total	1,637	934	2,571

Results achieved in these attacks.

	Battleships	Aircraft Carriers	Cruisers	Destroyers	Others
Sunk				9	4
Damaged	9	10	4	58	93

Total: Sunk: 13
        Damaged: 174

It goes without saying that we, the suicide-pilots, were not kept informed of these results, which were very modest in relation to the actual number of sorties.

results, since planes could no longer be spared to go out on checking-up missions.

Fujisaki too had died bravely! Next time, it would be my turn. In spite of myself, I felt a shiver run through me.

June 3.

Our suicide-attack training had just finished. For several days we had been in the underground shelters round the airfield, which we had built with the aid of the maintenance crews. The billets on the base were too vulnerable to American raids.

In the early afternoon, a happy surprise – my mother and two of my sisters came to visit me! I was dumbfounded for a moment. I thought my mother looked tired; no doubt feeding the family was a great worry to her. The country people were not very obliging and I felt sorry for her with all my heart. Doubtless, the haunting fear of my death added to her burdens. I, her only son, was soon to die. She was condemned to live on with her memories, whereas I, reduced to nothing, would feel neither pain nor joy, and would have no memories. In a sense, I was the luckier of the two.

My sisters questioned me anxiously: 'Are you too among the suicide-pilots?' I was disconcerted. It was better that my family should know nothing. I replied hastily that I was just an ordinary pilot.

'But why must the planes crash?' they pursued. 'Isn't it enough to drop the bombs?'

If I had gone into detailed explanations, I would have given myself away.

'Listen carefully,' I said. 'You have nothing but a stone in your hand. What is the best way to hit a tree? To throw it, and perhaps miss, or to place the stone on the tree yourself? Do you see?'

My mother had guessed. I watched her covertly. She was listening with downcast eyes. Again my sisters asked me: 'Well, then, you will soon have to take part in these attacks, won't you?'

'No,' I replied, being careful not to show any hesitation. 'It's such a skilled operation that it requires very experienced pilots. We haven't had enough training, we would fail.'

I saw a slight look of relief flicker over my mother's face. I went to fetch my diary and the tortoise-shell cigarette case my eldest sister had given me. I gave them these objects, as if I were bequeathing them to them after my death, saying as calmly as I could: 'Mother, here is my diary, it contains all my thoughts. If the C.O. read it, he would punish me severely. As for the cigarette case, please keep it safely for me till I come home, it's much too fragile to be kept here. Take care of these things for me.'

My mother nodded, apparently accepting the pretext. This would be our last meeting. I accompanied them as far as Kagohara station. On the platform, I studied their faces, engraving them on my heart. In my secret being, I was bidding them farewell. And instead of savouring these last moments, I began to be impatient for the train to arrive. This last tête-à-tête was too painful. Finally, the train drew out. I had to struggle to keep back my tears. A rapid military salute and then I left the station and made my way back along the path I had just walked down with my mother. I looked for the trace of her footprints.

June 23.
Grey skies this week; the rainy season is already upon us. Three days ago, the Grummans appeared over our base so suddenly that there was no time to sound the alert. A peasant was working in his field near our billets. We shouted to him: 'Look out! Take cover!' Too late: A Grumman dived down like a fierce bulldog rushing at a man. Its thick snout made me think of this snarling dog . . . Tak, tak tak! . . . and the old peasant crumpled up and did not move again. The enemy had shot down a civilian before our very eyes, a frightful spectacle that filled us with fury and disgust.

According to a reconnaissance report, the U.S. Task Force was within our range, off the coast of Miyagui. It had been raining since morning. The enemy fighters would hesitate to take off from the carriers in this bad weather. Shouldn't we take advantage of this? Destroying the American fleet was a prime necessity. In his rage at having witnessed the murder of a civilian, someone suggested we should ask the commandant to send us out on a sortie at once. We were all for it. He ran to convey our wishes to Flight Lieutenant Takagui, who went straight to the C.O. But a few minutes later he returned disappointed. 'No,' he said sullenly, 'the C.O. won't give the order. He says we'll never find the Task Force in this poor weather, and we can't risk using up our fuel on a useless mission. Be patient, that's what he says.'

We were disappointed. But we would be able to take advantage of any brightening of the weather in the next few days. Meanwhile, the rain confined us to our gloomy quarters. I suddenly felt a desire to re-read the *Les Maîtres Sonneurs*. I had not even had time to leaf through this work since Nozawa had been kind enough to bring it to me in Ozuki. Certainly I would not be able to finish it before I made my sortie, I knew that, but I took it out of my case and began reading it, anyway.

'Little Brulette had thus become Brulette the Beautiful, and was much talked of in the neighbourhood. Within living memory, no one could recall seeing a prettier girl, or one with finer eyes or rosier cheeks. She had the daintiest of figures, hair like spun gold, soft hands and a sweet little foot as small as a child's. . . .'

I longed to see my sisters growing up to be beautiful and graceful like Brulette – vain hope! The more I read, the more it confirmed my profound attachment to French literature. To sit quietly in my study and read all the works of George Sand before my life drew to its natural close, that seemed to me the peak of happiness. Alas! It was just a dream . . .

June 28.
For several hours, the commandant had been coming and going between the improvised meteorological station and his makeshift office, as if something exceptional was about to occur.

At 2000 hours, he ordered the twenty-two pilots to assemble. He made a solemn announcement:

'According to the met. report, we can expect some clear weather tomorrow morning off the coast near Miyagui, where the U.S. Fleet is. So this is the moment we have waited so eagerly. I am passing on to you the order to make a special attack sortie.'

In spite of my unshakable determination, I felt my heart turn over, and knew that I was deathly pale. I made an effort to recover from the shock. The words 'special attack' rang rather falsely. I felt I was living a nightmare. Suenaga consulted a sheet of paper he was holding. The dry crackle of the paper brought me back to earth.

'Here is the order,' he said. 'The *Kikusui* group will undertake the suicide-attack on the twenty-ninth of June, 1945.

Take-off at oh-six hundred hours. Objective: the Third Fleet of Task Force 38, composed of three aircraft carriers, two light aircraft carriers, three battleships, several cruisers, both heavy and light. They are situated three hundred and twelve miles off the coast in the region of Miyagui. Flight Leader: Flight Lieutenant Norio Takagui. Aim: to destroy the enemy ships. That is all!'

He paused briefly after reading the order. Then he said warmly: 'According to our information, this fleet posseses two important aircraft carriers, the *Essex* and the *Hancock*. These are the most vital ships to aim at. But don't quarrel amongst yourselves over the choice of prey. Just leave me one aircraft carrier for the day when I make my own sortie. Joking apart, make sure you go to bed early and get a good night's sleep. You will need to be extremely clear-headed on this mission. Dismissed!'

Returning to the dim-lit officers' billets, we sat about rather glumly on our beds. We felt, literally, the hand of death upon us. Just eleven hours left to live. It was in all our minds. Like the others, I was thinking: what is death? What is the source of our fear of it? Were we more afraid of the undoubted physical pain it would entail, or of the unknown world into which we would enter? Yet death would release us from all our earthly cares; shouldn't we look upon it, then, as a consolation? We often speak of freedom . . . the freedom of the individual, freedom of thought, freedom to work. . . . These are considered to be the basic rights of man. Nevertheless, in our society, we cannot really be said to enjoy them; man is under the yoke of money and of the authorities who rule him. To be free is to escape from all one's fetters. In life, this is impossible, but after death man enjoys perfect freedom. Why, then, is he so attached to his existence in this world, and why does he seek so earnestly to find a meaning in this life?

I was aware that I was doing the opposite: seeking a meaning and a justification for death, by negating the value of life. The imminent approach of death forced me to it. Moreover, mine would be a death totally unlike that caused by an illness, for example. I would have to be in a fit state to act with absolute lucidity right up to the last moment, whereas the mortally sick man is compelled to await death helplessly, on his bed, without taking any action. My own death had a significance, a purpose and a value. To my great astonishment, these reflections began

162

to relieve my mind after a while, and helped me to regain my tranquillity.

'Hey,' I said jokingly to Tanaka, 'you're a budding bonze, aren't you? The Buddhists say that anyone who has sinned is condemned to hell. Well now, we are about to carry out a massacre, but it is for our homeland, and therefore a virtuous act. Tell me, shall we go to heaven or to hell?'

'Ach, that's simple,' he replied with a forced smile, 'half our souls will go to hell and half to heaven.'

Everyone smiled. The tension dissipated. 'I'm going to write my will,' said someone. We approved of the idea.

I cut my nails and a lock from my hair. Then I settled down to write to my family but, when it came to it, I could not clarify my thoughts. It was hard to find words to express something that I felt so profoundly; I made vain efforts. On the other hand, memories of childhood and adolescence crowded in upon me: Mother taking care of me when I fell off my bicycle and hurt myself, walks with the whole family, seaside holidays, my mother giving my friends a warm welcome, my father's passion for sculpture, my mother and eldest sister serving me tea at midnight on the eve of my examinations, my parents' delight when I was accepted by the Shizuoka High School . . . endless recollections. . . . I took refuge in the pleasures of the past. Nine hours slipped by, and then . . .

My pen began to move over the page:

'My dear parents, I shall depart this life at 0700 hours on the twenty-ninth of June, 1945. My whole being is permeated by your tremendous affection, down to the last tiny hair. And it is this which is hard to accept: the thought that, with my carnal disappearance, this tenderness will also disappear. But patriotic duty demands it. I sincerely beg your pardon for not carrying out my filial duties to the very end. Please remember me to all those who have shown me friendship and kindness.

'Dear sisters, farewell! Our parents no longer have a son. It must therefore be your task to give them every loving care during their lifetime. Always be kind and gracious, worthy of Japanese womanhood.'

I would have liked to write a great deal more, but I contented myself with signing and adding the date: 'twenty-eighth of June, 1945. Twenty-two hundred hours.' I put my will, together with the paper containing my hair and nails, into an

163

envelope. As I sealed it, it occurred to me that everything was now over and done with.

As I lay in bed, my heart beat fit to burst with anguish. Other than the brotherhood of my fellow suicide-pilots, who could understand me? Actually, it mattered very little to me whether or not another could read my heart. The depths of human feeling are unsoundable. The mind of man functions mechanically at times, moved by force of circumstances, as if driven by an electric current, but it is too complex and mysterious to be understood solely in these terms.

The last night of my life passed like others before it. My sleep was a mere pause, like the sleep a pilot snatches between one battle and the next.

June 29, 0400 hours.
Time to get up. I put on clean underclothes. Then I made my bed and neatly laid out on it the belongings I was leaving for my family: uniform, cap, pen and paper. After a moment's hesitation, I wrote: 'The late Flight Lieutenant Ryuji Nagatsuka.' I placed this paper on my sword. We were forbidden to take swords into the cockpits of our planes as they might affect the gyroscope. In three hours' time, they would be lighting sticks of incense in front of these objects. This vision moved me, but I must admit it was nothing more than a sentimental notion, I was not really upset about it. A sort of resignation had taken possession of me. A French novelist, whose name escapes me, says that resignation is our daily suicide. Ah, well! A suicide-pilot has need of this kind of moral suicide.

Fear comes promptly, instantaneously. During the night, I had lain frozen and numb with terror in my bed. Yet even the fear of death becomes dulled in time. A few hours are enough to blunt it. The function of consciousness in man is truly inexplicable and time has magical powers. Without being clear as to why, I felt reasonably calm. I covertly watched my comrades who, like me, were putting their belongings in order. Some of them interrupted the task to plunge into meditation. They were steady, and sure of themselves. Perhaps, deeply hidden in their hearts, there was anguish at the imminence of death. But man's vanity is such that he will always act a part, right up till the end. When he stands with his back to the wall, all hope of escape gone, he unites himself mystically with death, instead of struggling like a madman, out of a sense of affinity.

0430 hours.
Day was breaking – a feeble grey dawn without benefit of sun. I ate my last breakfast: a bowl of *sekihan*, a cup of soup, a little dried fish, an egg. I glanced at my watch without thinking: 0440 hours. Once more, two figure four's, double symbol of death. At that instant, I clearly made out the black speck, image of my death, which I had not seen for quite a time. It seemed to be staring at me. But, for once, it was not threatening, it no longer worried me. I paid no more attention to it than if it were an optical illusion.

Still 1 hour and 20 minutes before the fateful moment of take-off. No, 80 minutes! It was 4,800 seconds! Now I was counting time in seconds, for I had the illogical feeling that 4,800 seconds were longer than 80 minutes. A delusion! I would have done better to take off my watch, perhaps. I no longer needed it, there was a chronometer on the instrument panel. This watch was a present from my mother, to celebrate my acceptance into the high school. Hastily, I returned to my room and laid it on my bed, amongst the objects to be left after my death. I took a photograph of my family and the two volumes of *Les Maîtres Sonneurs* out of my case and slipped them into the pockets of my summer suit. They would accompany me to the very end. Somehow, this comforted me. Was it just an affectation? I wanted to go to my death carrying those things that had been most dear to me: the faces of my loved ones, and the books that represented my passion for French literature.

Briefing was scheduled for 0500 hours. It took ten minutes to reach the briefing room at a run. Together with my comrades, I started off like an arrow.

0500 hours.
The horizon was growing lighter, but still the sky kept a greyish tinge. Low clouds covered it entirely. There was a threat of rain in the air. Soldiers in the meteorological service were shuttling to and fro incessantly, between the briefing room and their weather station. Apparently the sky was not so densely clouded off the coast in the region of Miyagui.

The ground crews were lined up in front of the hangars, together with the schoolboys who had been conscripted for work on the aerodrome. Mechanics were testing the motors of the planes lined up on the runway. The six Ki-43s and the sixteen Ki-27s seemed to be champing at the bit, like impatient horses under starter's orders. The *Kikusui* [Floating Chrysanthemum] group would fly in three formations: eight Ki-27s commanded by Flight Lieutenant Takagui, seven others under the orders of Flying Officer Enomoto and six Ki-43s under the command of Flight Sergeant Otomo. These six Ki-43s would be piloted by N.C.O.'s who were all more experienced than the officers. The voices of the meteorological servicemen and the throbbing of the engines were the only sounds to be heard.

At the last moment, the chief mechanic ran to the briefing room. In a loud voice, he reported that the engines of four Ki-27s were not working properly: some were sputtering dangerously and others were leaking petrol. They belonged to four of the officers. After a brief hesitation, the flight commander declared: 'Too bad! There will be only eighteen planes in this sortie!' I looked at the four unhappy officers; their faces expressed neither relief nor satisfaction, neither disappointment nor anger, they seemed to be deprived of all sensation. In a daze, they ran towards their planes.

0530 hours.
The engines could no longer be heard. A strange silence reigned. Eighteen suicide-pilots lined up in front of two rickety tables covered with a white cloth, on which were set out twenty small cups and a bottle of *saké*. Flight Lieutenant Uehara poured us each a little *saké*. At last, the departure ceremony for suicide-pilots! But it was extremely simple. Formerly, the commander-in-chief of the Army Air Force and officers of the General Staff would honour the men by their presence . . . but by now, the frequency of these sorties had rendered them commonplace. They were small beer.

'Now,' said our commandant in ringing tones, 'I have nothing more to ask of you but to die heroically for your country. I wish you success in this mission. Let us salute in the direction of the Imperial Palace.'

After emptying our cups, we saluted and bowed low towards the south. I did not think of the Emperor, not even for one second. My thoughs were elsewhere. I looked at the wild

166

flowers at my feet and said to myself, 'They still have the right to live, whereas I shall be dead in two or three hours! Why? My life will have been more fleeting than that of a humble blade of grass!'

Takagui ordered us to form a circle around him. The ground crews and the schoolboys sang a solemn song with many verses:

> After the battle, our corpses will be strewn
> On the green mountain slopes,
> Our corpses will rest at the bottom of the sea.
> We shall give our lives for His Majesty,
> We shall die without regrets.

The woeful dirge went straight to my heart, but I kept a tight rein on myself.

'Now listen carefully,' said Flight Lieutenant Takagui. 'The enemy ships are at a hundred and forty-four degrees twenty longitude east, and thirty-nine latitude north. As planned, we shall fly in three formations. Speed: One hundred and fifty to one hundred and eighty miles per hour. Altitude: forty-five hundred feet over land and a hundred and fifty over the sea. Attack procedure: the First and Second Formations will use the wave-hopping approach, the Third the high-altitude. Nevertheless, this may be modified by the actual situation as we find it: in the last resort, you may choose your own method of attack. Even if we are attacked by enemy fighters don't break formation. Always follow your flight leader! I am hoping this bad weather will prevent the fighters from coming out . . . Now, let us observe one minute's silence. Let each one of you turn towards his native region. And then, we will smoke a last cigarette together. . . . '

I tried to recall the faces of my mother and sisters. To my amazement, I could not do so. Everything was blurred. My agitated brain could no longer remember.

0550 hours.

After saluting my comrades and the airmen seeing us off, I walk towards my plane. The sound of my measured steps rings strangely. My Ki-27 seems to grow larger and larger. It is about to take me to my death, a death that is inevitable and predetermined. I begin to run. Why? To reach death faster? I feel lighter than usual and, in fact, I am not wearing a parachute this time. I settle into the cockpit, get out again and touch the ground; it has supported me for twenty-one years, I murmur my thanks to it. Never again will I be able to put my feet upon the earth. Each gesture is the last. My seat is covered with brilliant flowers; perhaps the schoolboys, with tears in their eyes, have put them there as a farewell gift, as if a member of their own family were involved. I am going to die in the flower of my youth: my plane is also my coffin. Fully resolved to sacrifice my life for my country, I summon all my courage. I lay my hands on the two pockets in my summer suit: I can feel the photograph of my family and the books by George Sand. Farewell, farewell, my family! Farewell, George Sand!

At precisely 0600 hours, Flight Lieutenant Takagui's plane takes off. The second plane . . . the third . . . we follow, in order. The formation changes course, heading northeast, without waggling our wings in token goodbye. It is forbidden on account of the weight of the plane: with a 550 pound bomb fixed to the fuselage, the Ki-27 weighs nearly 3,750 pounds and the Ki-43 about 5,500 pounds. The bomb is all black.

0650 hours.
We are flying over the sea at 155 m.p.h. I am piloting the fourth plane in the first formation. Our altitude is in the order of 325 feet. Above us, clouds obscure the sky. We must have flown over Utsunomiya at about 0615 hours, but the clouds were too thick to see either the town or the airfield belonging to our former flying school. Now and again, I get a glimpse of the choppy sea, but I cannot see the 3rd Formation.

Fear plagues me. I ask myself: 'Will I suffer at the moment of the explosion?' I answer at once: 'Ugh! It's not worth thinking about. The pain will last only a flash, perhaps a tenth of a second. . . . '

We continue flying in tight formation. Visibility is very poor. I keep my eyes glued to the flight leader's plane. The Rising Sun painted on his fuselage in the form of a red circle is veiled now and then by light cloud, which also hides the other planes from me. With their green and white patches, these fighters have a somewhat sorrowful air. In the sunshine, they might be compared to the swift little birds of Elysium, but at this moment, in their camouflage, they make me think of the

168

monstrous birds of hell. In spite of their speed, they look as if they are hanging motionless in the sky.

A curious image comes to mind: a dead Samurai, seen in a film when I was a child. Exposed to the glacial wind on the foggy and deserted banks of the river Styx, he had done his best to build a pile of stones, but the invisible demons of hell threw down his cairn before it could reach the required height. According to Buddhist legend, a dead man must construct a cairn of stones to gain the eternal repose of his soul: a virtuous soul will do so without difficulty, a man who has lived in vice will never succeed, for the demons will not let him.

Are mischievous fiends preventing our planes from reaching their target, as the Samurai was prevented from building his tower of stones in the film? Is our instinct for self-preservation unconsciously causing us to prolong this death flight? The engine throbs laboriously, perhaps on account of the heavy bomb-load. It seems to be grumbling as if it knows that, in less than eighty minutes, death will seize us by hook or by crook. In a quarter of an hour, it will be utterly impossible to return to base. I shall have no choice but to go on searching for enemy ships in this vile weather.

The sea below me is rough and grey. The high white waves are like fabulous beasts showing their teeth. But at least this is the manifestation of nature, of life, and when I consider that soon I shall have no contact with these things, I find the angry swell and the foam pleasing to the eye. I feel a profound attachment to life surging up anew within me, lacerating my heart, as death approaches closer and closer. I am fully conscious of it. I long to cry out: 'Why me? Why must I die, when my fellow-students are allowed to live, and will be able to resume their studies?' There is no answer, no solution. Man is too weak to accept an accomplished fact without regret.

But I am no longer a student, I am a suicide-pilot. I am about to crash-dive on the enemy without hope of return. What is the good of struggling with myself? I say resignedly: 'Farewell, nature! Farewell, world!'

0700 hours.

I turn to look at the fifth plane, piloted by Flying Officer Tanaka. He seems to be staring at me, but probably he is just looking at my plane so as to keep in close formation. Perhaps he is not even aware of me? His motionless profile, in the summer suit and dark-brown flying helmet, resembles a statue of Buddha in a dark temple. What is he thinking of? Undoubtedly, concentrating all his attention on the flight leader's aircraft.

In reality, one has no leisure to indulge in meditation during a special sortie, one must be constantly on the watch for enemy fighters, which may swoop out of the clouds at any point. By now, we must be within range of the American radar. If we sight an adversary it will already be too late! Since we are unarmed and have no means of defending ourselves, and since the American pilots are admittedly more skilful in battle than we are, they will shoot us down.

If, by good luck, I do not encounter any, all I have to do is skip over the waves, or dive down, and hit my target. It will be essential to hold the control column firmly so as to keep the plane steady and on course when it is shaken by ack-ack fire! Even if I am hit by bullets, even if one wing of the plane is torn off, I must hang on to that stick, so as to hit the American aircraft carrier fair and square! No one but myself will be aware of this act. My will, written last night in the underground shelter, and full of heart-rending words, will remain on this earth, either in my parents' keeping or in the library of my university. But only I can know what is passing through my mind now, during the time since I climbed into the suicide-plane. And I no longer have any means of communicating with others.

Suddenly, a feeling of terrifying solitude freezes my blood. Who is my companion at the last moment? Oh, what a mockery! A soulless metal object – the control column! At this thought, I grasp it more tightly in my gloved right hand as if it were a living thing. Yes, this is my last companion-in-eternity. My body will be shattered to pieces and, at the bottom of the sea, my right hand will hold fast to this companion in misfortune, without feeling the least hatred for the enemy.

Before long, I shall lose myself in the abyss of nothingness, where I shall see nothing, hear nothing, feel nothing. My parents would like to believe that my soul still exists, floating somewhere in the universe. Yet they too will enter into nothingness sooner or later, like me. After their death, all memory of me will disappear: the being known as Ryuji Nagatsuka will be totally effaced.

In spite of my efforts, I am suffering cruelly, as if from a

170

sly dagger thrust. It stems, not from fear of death or the desire to flee, but from the realisation that I shall have no one near me at that final moment. Self-respect demands that I keep my reason and control. At the moment of striking the enemy vessel, I must be able to say to myself: 'This is death,' instead of shouting: 'Long live the Emperor!' like a soldier drunk with emotion. The important thing is to know how to die. And this, too, causes me to suffer. Does my face betray this fearful inner struggle? The American attacks are like waves that beat incessantly on our shores, and I am nothing but a prop in the breakwater that strives to throw them back.

I am waiting to get a glimpse of the U.S. Fleet. . . . At the moment, our formations are flying through cotton wool. Rolling masses of thick cloud . . . and now rain lashes the windshield! That damned weather report! The position is really sticky. Yet, oddly enough, I feel on top of my form at last.

But can we locate the 38th Task Force in this weather? I am very doubtful. Our inadequate training makes it hard for us to fly in such poor visibility. Gaining altitude would mean a dangerous increase in fuel consumption. What is the flight leader going to do?

0705 hours.

Suddenly, Flight Lieutenant Takagui points to the rear. My God, there must be American planes pursuing us! I turn round: nothing. Nothing but thick cloud. Without a radio, I cannot understand the leader's signal.

A few seconds later, Takagui swings his plane round to the left. What, is he turning back?

'No, no! You can't want to go back?' I shout indignantly into the void. 'I know visibility's poor, and the enemy may still be a good hundred and fifty miles away, but . . . why this cowardice?'

Another 'I' speaks: 'He is right. Our mission is impossible under these conditions, so it's better to go back and wait for a better chance.'

Instinct and reason dispute with each other.

'Ugh!' I reply. 'How can you say it's impossible to find the enemy when we haven't even reached the zone where their ships are? If I can't find them, too bad! I'm not afraid to crash into the sea and die!'

'A pointless death,' says the other 'I'. 'It would be unthink-

171

able to waste a plane and a pilot for nothing, when the army is so short of them.'

Answer: 'Well, suppose we can't find the Task Force, surely we can catch *one ship* somewhere, out of all that great Fleet?'

'No, no,' protests the other voice. 'It's no use unless you can be certain of finding the enemy force. Better to turn back and await more favourable conditions.'

'But you know quite well our base has no more fuel, and nobody knows when we'll get any. So how can we be sure of carrying out another mission? This is our only chance. What ignominy to creep back like this, after vowing to sacrifice our lives! What will they say at the base?'

'Your life, too, is precious. Don't worry about what people will think. Aren't you a man of reason? Keep calm. Remember, the vital thing is to carry out a successful mission.'

'No, no! I must have the guts to go on alone, even if the leader turns back and my comrades follow him!'

'You're crazy! You know perfectly well you're not capable of acting on your own.'

The other 'I' is silent. He hesitates. My throat is constricted, I am panting with thirst. My whole body is on fire. Drops of sweat trickle down my nose and drip on to my lips; unthinkingly, I lick them. They taste salty and I make a sort of gurgling sound as I painfully swallow my saliva. So? Am I going to obey Flight Lieutenant Takagui's order to return, or carry on alone?

At that moment, I see the second and third planes swinging round obediently. My left foot presses the rudder pedal and my hand automatically tips the stick to change course.

In spite of that argumentative inner voice, I obey my flight leader. And I have to admit that he is right. There is not the slightest hope now that the skies will clear. It is more than 300 miles from our airfield to the objective, and they have given us only enough fuel for the outward journey: 330 miles. In ten minutes' time, it will be too late to return to base. The bomb fixed to the belly of the plane makes a forced landing utterly impossible. If we carry on flying through this cotton wool and fail to detect the U.S. Fleet, it will only mean throwing away our lives for nothing. Our flight leader must have reasoned it all out. I choke back my tears. No doubt my comrades are in the same state.

0730 hours.

The clouds cover the whole sky, like a great eiderdown. My plane flies beneath them with a continuous, rhythmic humming that seems to express a kind of relief. Beyond the clouds, death lay in wait for me, but I have just regained the hope of living here on earth for a little while longer. Should I thank the clouds, or curse them for preventing us from carrying out the mission?

The abyss retreats from view. This feeling of security regained disposes me to meditate on the great nothingness, like the child who is always eager to examine, from a safe distance, something which has frightened him. I had believed that nothingness was absolute non-being. Now, it may be that it resembles a universe without the limits of time and space, in which case it could still contain *being*, as the Buddhist bonzes claim, in their exalted mode of thought. Can it be that the oriental concept of death has penetrated my soul without my knowing it?

I feel as solitary and remote as if I were on the peak of a high mountain. But really, this solitude is superficial: as always, there are two Nagatsukas in me: one who bears the rank of flying officer and the other who has neither name nor title.

At the moment, Flying Officer Nagatsuka is hounding me with endless questions and reproaches: Why did you turn back? Don't you realise what punishments and humiliations will be waiting for you at the base? The ground crews, even the schoolboys will look at you coldly. You will suffer for yourself and for the others until the next sortie. A military pilot must respect honour before life. You will be nothing but a coward in the eyes of all personnel. Having agreed to sacrifice your life, you should have carried on till the end. If you plead the impossibility of locating the U.S. Fleet, without having pushed on into the zone where they were to be found, it will be just a feeble excuse. They will say you prefer to suffer mortification rather than die a hero. Shame on you!'

On the other hand, the student Nagatsuka, who is lurking in the depths of my heart, speaks up: 'It is destiny that has given me back to life, in spite of my decision. It is absurd to toy with life, which is the only thing in the world that really matters. Do I really believe in the efficacy of suicide-attacks? Aren't they basically foolhardy, since the missions are carried

173

out without fighter escort and in weaponless planes? Perhaps I have been convinced that it was the last and only means of defending my compatriots and saving Japan *against my better judgement*. The suicide-mission is senseless, although we are compelled to say "yes" to it. The soldiers at the base look at us with their eyes full of feeling, and we wave to them, but why don't we all admit that success is dubious and the whole mission an abominable deception? I did right to prize my life highly and turn back. Never mind the humiliation, it will only serve to make me more sure of myself in the end.'

Which is the real 'me'? I am suffocating. Stricken with despair, I would not need much persuasion to let the soldier Nagatsúka take over and fly back in search of the enemy. The student is right to restrain him: it is a lonely struggle in my innermost being, and no one can come to my aid . . .

When all is said and done, it is too late to change course again. I have not enough fuel to reach the zone where the U.S. ships are said to be. I try to disengage myself from the two Nagatsukas and concentrate on the landing, which will certainly be problematic. If I touch down with a jolt, there is a danger of setting off the bomb. That would indeed be a futile death! Can I land without disaster? Anxiety grips me as the airfield approaches.

0805 hours.
I can see the landing strip, wet with rain. Careful now! Gently, gently! I land with the utmost caution . . . then wait. Planes are landing one after the other. . . . Eleven, twelve . . . that's all. The six Ki-43s are not there. I am worried: didn't they all turn back with us?

Followed by eleven pilots, Flight Lieutenant Takagui reports to the commanding officer: 'Sir, I beg a thousand pardons,' he says in a mournful voice, 'mist and bad weather prevented our reaching the target. The Third Formation carried on in spite of my signal to return. It seems Flight Sergeant Otomo's radio was no longer working. He did not answer my call. That is all.'

We are lined up, our heads hanging, in front of the commandant, Suenaga. He says simply: 'It can't be helped. A pity, but you'll have another opportunity to destroy the aircraft carriers. Go to your quarters.'

Nevertheless, everyone stays under the awning outside the

briefing room in the hopes of seeing the six Ki-43s return. We look at one another in silence. Nothing can be heard but the hammering of the rain as it shakes the green canvas.

1000 hours.

For two hours, my comrades and I waited in vain for the return of the 3rd Formation. No message came from Otomo. If he had managed to locate the enemy fleet, he would have sent the message: 'Target sighted.' Knowing how little fuel the Ki-43s had, there could no longer be any doubt as to their fate. When the fuel ran out, they must have plunged into the sea, senselessly, without reaching their objective.

The faces and figures of all the N.C.O.'s who had not returned were vividly present in my mind: Otomo, robust as an ox; Leading Aircraftman Kanai with his cherubic, ever-smiling face; Leading Aircraftman Kishi, stubborn and a little defiant – before departure, he had looked at the C.O. with an expression that seemed to say: 'What do I care about the others! I shall go it alone!'

In no way did I feel that I had had a lucky escape, and still less did I feel any joy at finding myself alive and back at the base. I walked along the path leading to the underground shelters without bothering to avoid the puddles. My soul was empty of all feeling, I was so distracted that I did not know whether I was walking straight or staggering like a drunken man. Fields of wet corn stretched as far as the eye could see. I saw, without looking at it, this green carpet I had never thought to see again, but instead of being familiar, it had become almost hostile to me. Wasn't it reproaching me for the failure of the mission? This thought wrung my heart: the corn still had a right to exist, while I was nothing but a dead man who had been given a brief reprieve he did not even deserve. So others would judge me, they would say I had regained my life unjustly. My apparent good fortune had not saved me. No, I felt no joy. In the last analysis, I was indifferent to my fate.

I no longer grieved even for the tragic end of the N.C.O.'s, who must have perished in the sea, shedding tears of regret. I would certainly follow them to the grave as soon as more fuel was delivered to the base.

In front of the billets, the young officers of the 3rd Flight were waiting for me. They were former cadet pilots who had not yet been sent on a suicide-mission. I saluted them without a word. They returned my salute but said nothing. No doubt they were undecided whether to try and cheer me up or reproach me for cowardice: I believed I could read some compassion in their eyes . . . their turn would come, sooner or later. Their silence was rather consoling.

I went into one of the officers' rooms, a room in name only, for it was really a wretched cavern. My sword and the envelope containing my will were still on my bed. I had written: 'The late Flight Lieutenant Nagatsuka.' This paper filled me with disgust: it flaunted itself, it insulted me. In a fury, I tore it into a thousand pieces, then I cleared my bed. Nobody dared to speak. Even Flying Officer Tanaka, such a chatterbox as a rule, sat with his mouth shut. We were crushed with shame, remorse tormented us. Lying on my bed, I tried to doze, but it was no good. My mind was over-excited, but then a great physical and moral fatigue overwhelmed me. I tried to convince myself I had been the victim of circumstances beyond my control.

A few minutes later, we were summoned by the C.O. We found ourselves facing Suenaga and Flight Lieutenant Uehara. I looked for Takagui, but he was not there.

'You are the first special attack pilots of our squadron,' said the C.O., speaking tonelessly and trying to keep a check on his rage. 'Otomo, together with five other N.C.O.'s, pursued the mission to its conclusion, even though they were not lucky enough to sink any enemy ships. It is clear that they were ready for death before they took off. But you . . . you had not been able to prepare yourselves for it. This is proved by your cowardly return on the pretext of bad weather conditions. You funked it. . . . Those N.C.O.'s were imbued with ardent military spirit, but you have remained students. You have dishonoured our squadron and I am ashamed of you. You wasted our last remaining fuel. Because of your cowardice, the Twenty-fourth Squadron will be forced to reform as an infantry battalion. Why didn't you die like heroes?'

His lips trembled, we could hear him grinding his teeth.

What an irrational principle it was that, once the suicide-pilot had set out, he had no right whatever to return to base! Hadn't the very first suicide-pilot, Lieutenant Yukio Seki himself, come back three or four times before finally accomplishing his successful mission? The essence of the thing, surely, was not to die but to sink enemy ships under the most favourable conditions available. Commandant Suenaga was not unaware of this, and yet he was thinking of nothing but the honour of his squadron! His whole body shook with uncontrollable anger. Goaded by his own inner contradictions, he wanted to avenge himself on us. This made me furious. I would have liked to answer him: 'I am not afraid of death. It was Flight Lieutenant Takagui who ordered us to return. Aren't junior officers obliged to obey their superiors? Where is Takagui? Why don't you reproach him too? Your prejudice is intolerable.'

Twenty times I opened my mouth to speak, but I kept quiet. My insubordination would have been unworthy of a pilot.

At the time of our return to the airfield, our C.O. had been quiet lenient with us, now he was raging like a wild beast. What a change in behaviour! It baffled me, until an explanation suddenly occurred to me: 'Of course,' I said to myself, 'Takagui is a regular, professional airman from the military academy, like Suenaga himself. Suenaga showed us clemency at the airfield because Takagui was present. It is the deplorable cliquishness of the *zol*!'

'Shame on you!' shouted the C.O. in peroration. 'It is as if you had deserted in the face of the enemy. You have discredited the squadron and demoralised my men. . . . I am putting you under arrest. You will copy out the sacred words of the Emperor until further orders!'

What could we do except bear these insults and bow our heads? He stamped out of the room, his heels ringing on the floor.

Then Flight Lieutenant Uehara stepped forward and punched each of the eleven flying officers in the face. His eyes expressed an implacable hatred towards us; we had been promoted to our present rank in a short time, whereas he had had to wait years and years. . . . All his jealousy burst out now. The blow of his fist was not so painful as the blow to one's self-respect.

Before starting to copy out the Emperor's sacred words, I wrote in my diary all that had passed through my mind during my two hours' flight. No one would ever have known it, it was only by the most extraordinary mischance that I was able to record it. My intention was to communicate these thoughts to my parents and my intimate friends. The problem was, how to smuggle the diary out secretly.

Copying out the Emperor's sayings, I remembered the words of Lieutenant Yukio Seki, spoken just before he left on his last mission: 'It is not for the Emperor, nor for Japan, that I undertake this suicide-attack, but solely for my beloved wife.' I shared his sentiments. I too would have thought my death worthwhile if it saved my family and friends from being massacred by the Americans. My thoughts never, at any moment, turned to the Emperor, who, in any case, had closed his eyes when this rash and inhuman tactic had been described to him. Did the Emperor have any idea of what went on in the mind and feelings of a suicide-pilot? Still less did he know about the insults to which pilots who returned to base were subjected. I would have liked to cry out to him: 'Look at me, wasting time copying out these hollow phrases! To hell with it! Give me some fuel and good weather, not your words! I would set out this minute on a suicide-mission to defend my family and my country, but I do not want to die for a man who calls himself Emperor!'

This cry from the heart expressed a rage I could not vent on anyone, as well as a violent protest against the arbitrary actions of the *zol*, for they despised men and treated them like cattle, all in the name of the Emperor.

The days of our arrest followed one another in dreary, monotonous procession. Plunged into gloom and appalling apathy, I spent them growling to myself at the indignity of our treatment. To a man like myself, proud of being an officer, it was hellish and infinitely humiliating. Sitting with us, Takagui also wasted his time copying passages from the Emperor's rescript. What was he thinking? I was more interested in trying to divine what had been the intimate feelings of the six N.C.O.'s who had chosen to die for no purpose. Why? If they had survived that day, they would have had death forced upon them sooner or later, anyway. Perhaps they had preferred to die with good grace rather than return to undergo the profound and futile misery which was our lot. They must have foreseen it, and, having suffered the absurdities of war, they had somehow come to look upon death as a deliverance.

Must I die, then, without accomplishing my mission, in order to save the honour of the squadron, as the commandant claimed? Did he really put the squadron's reputation before the lives of his men?

We were released after three days. There was still no fuel at the base and the sky was still blanketed with very low cloud. It was several days before we began to see an improvement in the weather. Far from grieving me, the possibility of soon taking off for the fatal flight brought me joy. Alas! On July 18, we heard some exasperating news: Task Force 38 was heading southeast. Soon, it would be out of our range. Other groups would be entrusted with the suicide-attacks. I was in despair, for all my inner struggles to reach the point where I could accept a patriot's death would be null and void.

We were expecting to see the Americans invade our own territory: the Japanese Archipelago. The General Staff ordered pilots who were without fuel to take part in infantry training. They must learn to attack tanks. Pilots turned into foot-sloggers! With heavy hearts, we joined the ground crews in these exercises, which went on all day long, but the was no zeal in it.

Silent and sullen, Flight Lieutenant Takagui made no attempt to hide his wrath, his melancholy and his shame. Like him, we were all on the rack. I had the impression that the mechanics looked at us with limitless contempt, as if reproaching us for cowardice, but perhaps this was just my imagination.

At the moment when I turned back, I had moved the rudder bar and the control column unconsciously – though not without a brief hesitation – to follow my flight leader. Did this instinctive gesture betray my true cowardice? Is a desire to avoid a pointless death the same as cowardice? Tormented, I could no longer read my own heart clearly. I did not even have the energy to write to my parents any more.

At the end of July, fuel was at last issued to the 24th Squadron. We were joyful at the chance to retrieve the lost mission. Was my motivation patriotic zeal or the desire to wipe out my shame? The air force officer was gaining on the student.

The U.S. Fleet was still beyond our range. Flight Lieutenant Takagui, followed by eleven flying officers, asked the C.O. to transfer us to another base, one from which we would be able to reach the objectives. Our request was refused: our fuel was to be reserved for engagements with enemy aircraft.

On August 6, the atomic bomb was dropped on Hiroshima. On August 8, Russia declared war on Japan. The atomic attack

179

on Nagasaki came on August 9. Our chances of carrying a final victory had well and truly evaporated.

Suddenly, on the evening of August 12, the alert sounded: American fighters were about to invade the air space over Kanto. All pilots ran to the airfield. Since the squadron had received fuel, anti-tank training had ceased and ground and air crews were on the alert every day.

In the briefing room, I listened nostalgically to the throbbing of the Ki-43 engines. The setting sun still bathed the runway in its light. Twilight would come much later. The C.O. looked over the pilots lined up before him. I looked into his eyes, silently asking to be numbered amongst the pilots who would go into action. As if he had understood me, he announced: Flight Lieutenant Takagui, Flying Officer Hiraga, Flying Officer Nagatsuka . . . ' There were only six Ki-43s left at our base. I could feel how taut the muscles of my face were.

'Now,' declared Suenaga, 'the American fighters are heading towards Kumagaya, to bomb the city. Bring down as many as you can to avenge in advance all the unlucky victims of to-night's air raid. Be fierce and daring! Scramble!'

Our six Ki-43s flew over the plain to the south of Kumagaya at an altitude of 6,500 feet – ten miles southeast of Kagohara. The horizon, massed with small clouds, was deep crimson. Suddenly, about 2,500 feet below me, I noticed little grey specks. Japanese planes from another squadron? No, they were Grummans, not the slightest doubt of it. I counted them . . . two, three, four, five . . . 'Let this be the battle to avenge the deaths of Tanizaki and the six N.C.O.'s of the *Kikusui* [Floating Chrysanthemums] special attack group!' I said to myself.

The enemy fighters seemed not to have noticed our presence. Takagui gave the signal to fan out.

Before dropping down to the attack, I looked round automatically. At once, several Grummans burst through the clouds some thousand feet away from me. They were charging at us. Damn! I hesitated a second: should I zoom climb or dive down to attack the other planes beneath me? I pressed the rudder bar to the left. A spiral dive. One of the American fighters dogged me stubbornly, I was within range of his machine guns, . . . a shiver of terror ran through my body.

I executed a series of barrel rolls to throw off my adversary and let him get clear. But two can play that game, and the American was not to be caught. He was still on my tail. His ice-candies grazed my plane . . . a few seconds later, my body suffered a violent shock, as if someone had hit me with a bludgeon. My right arm hung completely inert, and I saw blood rapidly staining my summer suit at the level of the shoulder. At once, my mind clouded.

For how long? . . . A flash of lightning in which I glimpsed the faces of my parents: my father was looking at me with unusual gravity and my mother was on the point of tears. Suddenly, I came to myself. My plane, off balance, was falling in a spin. I pulled the stick against my stomach with all my strength. Altitude: 3,000 feet! My enemy had vanished, he must have thought he had succeeded in shooting me down. My paralysed arm prevented me from rejoining the battle. Besides, for some unknown reason, my right leg was swollen. With rage and frustration in my heart, I decided to make a forced landing.

The last rays of the setting sun . . . 600 feet . . . 300 feet. . . . It seemed to me that another pilot, not I, was piloting the plane. My mind was seething with anxiety: I made an effort to put down the landing gear. A red bulb lit up to the left of the instrument panel. The mechanism, hit by bullets, would not function. No choice! I made a forced landing in a paddy field: I felt a jolt and immediately lost consciousness.

When I came to next day, I was in a hospital bed in a remote village. I was no longer capable of thought: a penetrating pain, aggravated by the intense heat of summer, dulled my mind.

At midday on August 15, I heard the Emperor's address on the radio. He spoke in a faint, indistinct voice. The Japanese nation heard him for the first time. Alas! Our country had suffered a total defeat. What thoughts came in those distressing hours! Had I effectively contributed to the defence of my country? I had not been able to shoot down either the B-29 or the Grumman; I had failed in my suicide-mission . . . and I was seriously wounded! After my return to the base, life had been nothing but humiliation. Perhaps the Emperor would announce his abdication, as a sign that he took responsibility for the defeat. . . . And what must I do now?

Waves of frustration, shame, rage, despair, washed over me. Incapable of thinking lucidly, I sank into a kind of stupor.

One Sunday in December, I arrived on the doorstep of the house my family was temporarily occupying, not far from Nagoya. My parents, my eldest sister and three little sisters,

Nobuko, Shigueko and Eiko, were all there. My sisters stared at me fixedly. Was it joy, or were they stunned at the sight of the wound that deprived me of the use of my right arm and leg? I saw my eldest sister's eyes fill with tears; she hurried away into another room to hide them.

. My mother's face looked just as I had imagined it when my plane was hurtling down. She smiled through her tears and all her maternal affection was revealed in that faint and timid smile.

'Well, come in!' said my father in a voice full of emotion.

In one room, I saw my bookcase in perfect order. On my desk lay the two volumes of *Les Maîtres Sonneurs*, my sword, the envelope containing my will and the diaries I had kept in the army. I was astonished.

'We know everything,' said my father. 'Your comrade, Flying Officer Tanaka, was kind enough to bring us your belongings on his way home.'

General MacArthur had ordered the Japanese military high command to demobilise all pilots as quickly as possible. My comrades in the 24th Squadron had left the base on the 20th of August.

'At last,' said my father, 'the war is behind us. Let's forget it all and never talk of it again! The important thing is we're alive.'

'Look,' said my mother, holding out a dictionary. 'The *Nouveau Petit Larousse Illustré*, 1940. I have always taken good care of your books. They were more important to us than the furniture. You will be able to go back to your studies. Are you pleased?'

'Thank you!' I said, bowing to them, too overcome to say anything more.

My left hand unconsciously stroked the two volumes of George Sand and the French dictionary. Assailed by a thousand sentiments, I would have liked to fall asleep in my mother's arms, serenely, as if I had still been a child.

Appendix: Statistics:
Suicide-Planes and Results Claimed

1. The Philippines

Date	No. of Planes	Results
October, 1944		
21	2	Uncertain
23	2	Uncertain
25	18	7 aircraft carriers damaged, 1 aircraft carrier and 1 light cruiser sunk
26	5	1 aircraft carrier damaged
27	11	Uncertain
28	1	1 light cruiser damaged
29	10	1 aircraft carrier damaged
30	6	3 aircraft carriers damaged
November, 1944		
1	8	1 destroyer sunk, 3 destroyers damaged
5	5	1 aircraft carrier damaged
6	6	
11	6	
12	25	2 small ships damaged
13	9	
14	2	
18	5	
19	8	
21	3	
24	3	
25	24	4 aircraft carriers damaged
26	7	

27	26	1 submarine chaser sunk, 1 battleship and 2 light cruisers damaged
29	6	1 battleship and 2 destroyers damaged

December, 1944

4	2	
5	19	2 destroyers, 1 steamboat and 3 small ships damaged
6	4	
7	45	1 destroyer sunk, 1 destroyer, 2 transport ships and 2 small ships damaged
8	2	
10	13	1 destroyer damaged and 1 torpedo boat sunk
11	10	1 destroyer and 1 small ship sunk, 1 destroyer damaged
13	9	1 destroyer and 1 light cruiser damaged
14	34	
15	24	2 small ships sunk, 1 aircraft carrier, 2 destroyers and 1 torpedo boat damaged
16	20	
17	3	1 torpedo boat damaged
18	8	1 torpedo boat damaged
21	7	2 small ships sunk, 1 destroyer and 1 transport ship damaged
22	3	1 destroyer damaged
25	2	
26	3	
28	4	1 petrol tanker and 2 cargo boats sunk
29	16	
30	4	1 destroyer and 1 special mission ship sunk, 1 destroyer and 1 special mission ship damaged

January, 1945

3	3	1 supply ship damaged

4	6	1 aircraft carrier and 1 supply ship sunk
5	39	2 aircraft carriers, 2 heavy cruisers, 2 destroyers, 2 seaplane carriers, 1 minesweeper, 1 landing craft and 1 small ship damaged
6	29	1 destroyer sunk, 2 battleships, 3 heavy cruisers, 1 light cruiser, 7 destroyers, 1 mine-sweeper, 1 transport ship and 1 seaplane carrier damaged
7	14	1 transport ship and 1 small ship damaged
8	10	2 aircraft carriers damaged
9	10	1 battleship, 2 cruisers and 1 destroyer damaged

2. Iwo Jima and at sea off Kyushu

January, 1945

4	4	
5	4	
6	3	
7	2	
8	9	
9	1	
10	6	
11	24	
12	29	
13	5	
15	8	
18	1	
21	21	2 aircraft carriers and 1 destroyer damaged
25	2	

February, 1945

21	12	1 aircraft carrier sunk, 2 aircraft carriers, 2 transport ships and 2 small ships damaged

185

March, 1945

1	1
21	36

3. Okinawa

February, 1945

11	24	1 aircraft carrier damaged
18	32	3 aircraft carriers damaged
19	19	2 aircraft carriers damaged
20	20	1 destroyer and 1 submarine damaged
21	15	
24	4	
25	8	2 destroyers and 1 transport ship damaged
26	14	1 battleship, 1 light cruiser, 5 destroyers and 1 minelayer damaged
27	26	2 destroyers damaged
28	5	
29	12	
31	5	

April, 1945

1	34	1 battleship, 2 destroyers, 3 transport ships, 2 aircraft carriers and 2 small ships damaged
2	51	4 transport ships and 1 small ship damaged
3	79	1 aircraft carrier and 1 destroyer damaged
4	6	1 transport ship sunk
5	3	
6	255	3 destroyers, 2 supply ships and 1 small ship sunk, 1 aircraft carrier, 12 destroyers and 4 mine-sweepers damaged
7	78	1 aircraft carrier, 1 battleship, 2 destroyers and 1 special mission ship damaged
8	11	1 destroyer damaged

4. 'Kikusui 2' Operation

April, 1945

9	6	1 destroyer damaged
10	1	
11	73	1 battleship, 1 aircraft carrier and 3 destroyers damaged
12	153	1 destroyer and 1 landing craft sunk, 2 battleships and 4 destroyers damaged
13	17	1 destroyer damaged
14	22	1 battleship and 2 destroyers damaged
15	2	2 destroyers damaged

5. 'Kikusui 3' Operation

April, 1945

16	191	1 destroyer sunk, 1 aircraft carrier, 1 battleship, 6 destroyers, 1 supply ship, 2 landing craft and 1 small ship damaged
17	30	1 destroyer damaged
18	3	
22	79	4 destroyers and 2 minesweepers damaged
23	2	

6. 'Kikusui 4-10 Operation
and at sea off the Nipponese Archipelago

April, 1945

26	2	1 supply ship sunk
27	27	2 destroyers damaged
28	85	5 destroyers, 1 transport ship and 1 hospital ship damaged
29	52	4 destroyers damaged

May, 1945

1	2	1 destroyer and 1 landing craft sunk
1	2	

3	12	1 destroyer and 1 landing craft sunk, 4 destroyers and 1 transport ship damaged
4	144	2 destroyers and 2 landing craft sunk, 3 aircraft carriers, 1 light cruiser, 5 destroyers, 1 mine-sweeper, 2 special mission ships and 1 small ship damaged
6	11	1 aircraft carrier and 1 survey vessel damaged
9	17	2 destroyers sunk, 2 aircraft carriers damaged
10	10	2 destroyers damaged
11	49	1 aircraft carrier, 3 destroyers and 1 steamship damaged
12	4	1 battleship damaged
13	13	2 destroyers damaged
14	9	1 aircraft carrier damaged
17	8	1 destroyer damaged
18	12	1 destroyer damaged
20	14	3 destroyers and 1 small ship damaged
21	7	
24	49	1 destroyer sunk, 5 destroyers and 1 mine-sweeper damaged, 29 aircraft destroyed and 70,000 gallons of petrol lost
25	118	1 destroyer sunk, 2 destroyers damaged
26	7	4 destroyers and 1 survey vessel damaged
27	34	1 destroyer sunk, 3 destroyers, 1 mine-sweeper and 2 transport ships damaged
28	66	1 destroyer sunk
29	7	1 destroyer damaged
31	1	

June, 1945

1	5	
3	33	1 transport ship damaged

5	4	1 battleship and 1 heavy cruiser damaged
6	35	1 aircraft carrier and 3 destroyers damaged
7	13	1 destroyer damaged
8	13	
10	2	1 destroyer sunk
11	12	
21	23	1 landing craft and 1 decoy ship sunk, 1 destroyer and 2 seaplane carriers damaged
22	37	1 destroyer and 1 small ship damaged
25	11	
26	14	
27	1	
28	1	
29	6	

July, 1945

1	2	
3	1	
19	6	1 destroyer damaged
25	12	

August, 1945

9	27	1 destroyer damaged
11	5	
13	8	1 transport ship damaged
15	19	1 seaplane carrier damaged

(Vice-Admiral Ugaki took part in this last sortie.)

HIMMLER
by Roger Manvell
and Heinrich Fraenkel

Heinrich Himmler became the most hated and feared of
the Nazi leaders – for it was in his activities as head of
the S.S. that Nazism found its most complete expression.
Yet his character was strangely at variance with his
political role: he was unassuming, pedantic and dull.
How, then, could he have been responsible for the mass
murder of European Jews and the terrible cruelties which
accompanied it?

This is the essential contradiction that the authors
reconcile in their masterly biography. Drawing on
hitherto unpublished documents, interviews with his
family, friends, members of staff and the S.S. they show
how Himmler's intensely superstitious nature led him
to adopt many eccentric beliefs, culminating in the most
dangerous of all – the superiority of the Aryan peoples.

'Anyone who wishes to study the great German aberration
can have a field-day with Heinrich Himmler, the latest
book by two talented authors.'

The Times

NEW ENGLISH LIBRARY

NEL BESTSELLERS

Crime

T013 332	CLOUDS OF WITNESS	*Dorothy L. Sayers*	40p
T016 307	THE UNPLEASANTNESS AT THE BELLONA CLUB	*Dorothy L. Sayers*	40p
T021 548	GAUDY NIGHT	*Dorothy L. Sayers*	40p
T026 698	THE NINE TAILORS	*Dorothy L. Sayers*	50p
T026 671	FIVE RED HERRINGS	*Dorothy L. Sayers*	50p
T015 556	MURDER MUST ADVERTISE	*Dorothy L. Sayers*	40p

Fiction

T018 520	HATTER'S CASTLE	*A. J. Cronin*	75p
T013 944	CRUSADER'S TOMB	*A. J. Cronin*	60p
T013 936	THE JUDAS TREE	*A. J. Cronin*	50p
T015 386	THE NORTHERN LIGHT	*A. J. Cronin*	50p
T026 213	THE CITADEL	*A. J. Cronin*	80p
T027 112	BEYOND THIS PLACE	*A. J. Cronin*	60p
T016 609	KEYS OF THE KINGDOM	*A. J. Cronin*	50p
T027 201	THE STARS LOOK DOWN	*A. J. Cronin*	90p
T018 539	A SONG OF SIXPENCE	*A. J. Cronin*	50p
T001 288	THE TROUBLE WITH LAZY ETHEL	*Ernest K. Gann*	30p
T003 922	IN THE COMPANY OF EAGLES	*Ernest K. Gann*	30p
T023 001	WILDERNESS BOY	*Stephen Harper*	35p
T017 524	MAGGIE D	*Adam Kennedy*	60p
T022 390	A HERO OF OUR TIME	*Mikhail Lermontov*	45p
T025 691	SIR, YOU BASTARD	*G. F. Newman*	40p
T022 536	THE HARRAD EXPERIMENT	*Robert H. Rimmer*	50p
T022 994	THE DREAM MERCHANTS	*Harold Robbins*	95p
T023 303	THE PIRATE	*Harold Robbins*	95p
T022 968	THE CARPETBAGGERS	*Harold Robbins*	£1.00
T016 560	WHERE LOVE HAS GONE	*Harold Robbins*	75p
T023 958	THE ADVENTURERS	*Harold Robbins*	£1.00
T025 241	THE INHERITORS	*Harold Robbins*	90p
T025 276	STILETTO	*Harold Robbins*	50p
T025 268	NEVER LEAVE ME	*Harold Robbins*	50p
T025 292	NEVER LOVE A STRANGER	*Harold Robbins*	90p
T022 226	A STONE FOR DANNY FISHER	*Harold Robbins*	80p
T025 284	79 PARK AVENUE	*Harold Robbins*	75p
T025 187	THE BETSY	*Harold Robbins*	80p
T020 894	RICH MAN, POOR MAN	*Irwin Shaw*	90p

Historical

T022 196	KNIGHT WITH ARMOUR	*Alfred Duggan*	50p
T022 250	THE LADY FOR RANSOM	*Alfred Duggan*	50p
T015 297	COUNT BOHEMOND	*Alfred Duggan*	50p
T017 958	FOUNDING FATHERS	*Alfred Duggan*	50p
T017 753	WINTER QUARTERS	*Alfred Duggan*	50p
T021 297	FAMILY FAVOURITES	*Alfred Duggan*	50p
T022 625	LEOPARDS AND LILIES	*Alfred Duggan*	60p
T019 624	THE LITTLE EMPERORS	*Alfred Duggan*	50p
T020 126	THREE'S COMPANY	*Alfred Duggan*	50p
T021 300	FOX 10: BOARDERS AWAY	*Adam Hardy*	35p

Science Fiction

T016 900	STRANGER IN A STRANGE LAND	*Robert Heinlein*	75p
T020 797	STAR BEAST	*Robert Heinlein*	35p
T017 451	I WILL FEAR NO EVIL	*Robert Heinlein*	80p
T026 817	THE HEAVEN MAKERS	*Frank Herbert*	35p
T027 279	DUNE	*Frank Herbert*	90p
T022 854	DUNE MESSIAH	*Frank Herbert*	60p
T023 974	THE GREEN BRAIN	*Frank Herbert*	35p
T012 859	QUEST FOR THE FUTURE	*A. E. Van Vogt*	35p

T015 270	THE WEAPON MAKERS	A. E. Van Vogt	30p
T023 265	EMPIRE OF THE ATOM	A. E. Van Vogt	40p
T017 354	THE FAR-OUT WORLDS OF		
	A. E. VAN VOGT	A. E. Van Vogt	40p

War

T027 066	COLDITZ: THE GERMAN STORY	Reinhold Eggers	50p
T009 890	THE K BOATS	Don Everett	30p
T020 854	THE GOOD SHEPHERD	C. S. Forester	35p
T012 999	P.Q. 17 – CONVOY TO HELL	Lund & Ludlam	30p
T026 299	TRAWLERS GO TO WAR	Lund & Ludlam	50p
T010 872	BLACK SATURDAY	Alexander McKee	30p
T020 495	ILLUSTRIOUS	Kenneth Poolman	40p
T018 032	ARK ROYAL	Kenneth Poolman	40p
T027 198	THE GREEN BERET	Hilary St George Saunders	50p
T027 171	THE RED BERET	Hilary St George Saunders	50p

Western

T016 994	EDGE No 1: THE LONER	George Gilman	30p
T024 040	EDGE No 2: TEN THOUSAND DOLLARS		
	AMERICAN	George Gilman	35p
T024 075	EDGE No 3: APACHE DEATH	George Gilman	35p
T024 032	EDGE No 4: KILLER'S BREED	George Gilman	35p
T023 990	EDGE No 5: BLOOD ON SILVER	George Gilman	35p
T020 002	EDGE No 14: THE BIG GOLD	George Gilman	30p

General

T017 400	CHOPPER	Peter Cave	30p
T022 838	MAMA	Peter Cave	35p
T021 009	SEX MANNERS FOR MEN	Robert Chartham	35p
T019 403	SEX MANNERS FOR ADVANCED LOVERS	Robert Chartham	30p
T023 206	THE BOOK OF LOVE	Dr David Delvin	90p
P002 368	AN ABZ OF LOVE	Inge & Stan Hegeler	75p
P011 402	A HAPPIER SEX LIFE	Dr Sha Kokken	70p
W24 79	AN ODOUR OF SANCTITY	Frank Yerby	50p
W28 24	THE FOXES OF HARROW	Frank Yerby	50p

Mad

S006 086	MADVERTISING	40p
S006 292	MORE SNAPPY ANSWERS TO STUPID QUESTIONS	40p
S006 425	VOODOO MAD	40p
S006 293	MAD POWER	40p
S006 291	HOPPING MAD	40p

NEL P.O. BOX 11, FALMOUTH, CORNWALL.

For U.K. & Eire: customers should include to cover postage, 15p for the first book plus 5p per copy for each additional book ordered, up to a maximum charge of 50p.

For Overseas customers & B.F.P.O.: customers should include to cover postage, 20p for the first book and 10p per copy for each additional book.

Name ....

Address..

....

Title ....
(MAY)